THE ADVENTURES OF TOM SAWYER

Mark Twain

SPARK PUBLISHING

SPARKNOTES is a registered trademark of SparkNotes LLC

Spark Publishing
A Division of Barnes & Noble
120 Fifth Avenue
New York, NY 10011
www.sparknotes.com

ISBN-13: 978-1-4114-0376-5
ISBN-10: 1-4114-0376-2

Please submit changes or report errors to www.sparknotes.com/errors.

Printed in the United States.

10 9 8 7 6 5 4 3 2 1

Contents

CONTEXT

MARK TWAIN WAS BORN Samuel Langhorne Clemens in Florida, Missouri, in 1835, and grew up in nearby Hannibal, a small Mississippi River town. Hannibal would become the model for St. Petersburg, the fictionalized setting of Twain's two most popular novels, *The Adventures of Tom Sawyer* and *The Adventures of Huckleberry Finn*. The young Clemens grew up in a prosperous family—his father owned a grocery store as well as a number of slaves—but he was sent out to work at the age of twelve after his father's death. As a young man, he traveled frequently, working as a printer's typesetter and as a steamboat pilot. In this latter profession he gained familiarity with the river life that would furnish much material for his writing. He also gained his pen name, Mark Twain, which is a measure of depth in steamboat navigation.

Twain enlisted in the Confederate militia in 1861, early in the Civil War, but he soon left to pursue a career in writing and journalism in Nevada and San Francisco. His articles and stories became immensely popular in the decades that followed. On the strength of this growing literary celebrity and financial success, he moved east in the late 1860s and married Olivia Langdon, the daughter of a prominent Elmira, New York, family. Twain and Langdon settled in Hartford, Connecticut; there Twain wrote *The Adventures of Tom Sawyer,* which he published in 1876. Twain proceeded to write, among other things, *The Adventures of Huckleberry Finn* (1884) and two sequels to *The Adventures of Tom Sawyer*: *Tom Sawyer Abroad* (1894) and *Tom Sawyer, Detective* (1896). He died in 1910, one of America's most beloved humorists and storytellers.

While *The Adventures of Tom Sawyer* retains some of the fragmented, episodic qualities of Twain's earlier, shorter pieces, the novel represents, in general, a significant literary departure for Twain. He toned down the large-scale social satire that characterized many of his earlier works, choosing instead to depict the sustained development of a single, central character. Twain had originally intended for the novel to follow Tom into adulthood and conclude with his return to St. Petersburg after many years away. But he was never able to get his hero out of boyhood, however, and the novel ends with its protagonist still preparing to make the transition into adult life.

Twain based *The Adventures of Tom Sawyer* largely on his personal memories of growing up in Hannibal in the 1840s. In his preface to the novel, he states that "[m]ost of the adventures recorded in this book really occurred" and that the character of Tom Sawyer has a basis in "a combination . . . of three boys whom I knew." Indeed, nearly every figure in the novel comes from the young Twain's village experience: Aunt Polly shares many characteristics with Twain's mother; Mary is based on Twain's sister Pamela; and Sid resembles Twain's younger brother, Henry. Huck Finn, the Widow Douglas, and even Injun Joe also have real-life counterparts, although the actual Injun Joe was more of a harmless drunk than a murderer.

Unlike Twain's later masterpiece, *The Adventures of Huckleberry Finn*, *The Adventures of Tom Sawyer* concerns itself primarily with painting an idyllic picture of boyhood life along the Mississippi River. Though Twain satirizes adult conventions throughout *The Adventures of Tom Sawyer*, he leaves untouched certain larger issues that *The Adventures of Huckleberry Finn* explores critically. *The Adventures of Tom Sawyer* never deals directly with slavery, for example, and, while the town's dislike of Injun Joe suggests a kind of small-town xenophobia (fear of foreigners or outsiders), Injun Joe's murders more than justify the town's suspicion of him. Because it avoids explicit criticism of racism, slavery, and xenophobia, the novel has largely escaped the controversy over race and language that has surrounded *The Adventures of Huckleberry Finn* in the twentieth and twenty-first centuries. To this day, *The Adventures of Tom Sawyer* remains perhaps the most popular and widely read of all Twain's works.

PLOT OVERVIEW

N IMAGINATIVE AND MISCHIEVOUS BOY named Tom Sawyer lives with his Aunt Polly and his half-brother, Sid, in the Mississippi River town of St. Petersburg, Missouri. After playing hooky from school on Friday and dirtying his clothes in a fight, Tom is made to whitewash the fence as punishment on Saturday. At first, Tom is disappointed by having to forfeit his day off. However, he soon cleverly persuades his friends to trade him small treasures for the privilege of doing his work. He trades these treasures for tickets given out in Sunday school for memorizing Bible verses and uses the tickets to claim a Bible as a prize. He loses much of his glory, however, when, in response to a question to show off his knowledge, he incorrectly answers that the first two disciples were David and Goliath.

Tom falls in love with Becky Thatcher, a new girl in town, and persuades her to get "engaged" to him. Their romance collapses when she learns that Tom has been "engaged" before—to a girl named Amy Lawrence. Shortly after being shunned by Becky, Tom accompanies Huckleberry Finn, the son of the town drunk, to the graveyard at night to try out a "cure" for warts. At the graveyard, they witness the murder of young Dr. Robinson by the Native American "half-breed" Injun Joe. Scared, Tom and Huck run away and swear a blood oath not to tell anyone what they have seen. Injun Joe blames his companion, Muff Potter, a hapless drunk, for the crime. Potter is wrongfully arrested, and Tom's anxiety and guilt begin to grow.

Tom, Huck, and Tom's friend Joe Harper run away to an island to become pirates. While frolicking around and enjoying their newfound freedom, the boys become aware that the community is sounding the river for their bodies. Tom sneaks back home one night to observe the commotion. After a brief moment of remorse at the suffering of his loved ones, Tom is struck by the idea of appearing at his funeral and surprising everyone. He persuades Joe and Huck to do the same. Their return is met with great rejoicing, and they become the envy and admiration of all their friends.

Back in school, Tom gets himself back in Becky's favor after he nobly accepts the blame for a book that she has ripped. Soon Muff Potter's trial begins, and Tom, overcome by guilt, testifies against

Injun Joe. Potter is acquitted, but Injun Joe flees the courtroom through a window.

Summer arrives, and Tom and Huck go hunting for buried treasure in a haunted house. After venturing upstairs they hear a noise below. Peering through holes in the floor, they see Injun Joe enter the house disguised as a deaf and mute Spaniard. He and his companion, an unkempt man, plan to bury some stolen treasure of their own. From their hiding spot, Tom and Huck wriggle with delight at the prospect of digging it up. By an amazing coincidence, Injun Joe and his partner find a buried box of gold themselves. When they see Tom and Huck's tools, they become suspicious that someone is sharing their hiding place and carry the gold off instead of reburying it.

Huck begins to shadow Injun Joe every night, watching for an opportunity to nab the gold. Meanwhile, Tom goes on a picnic to McDougal's Cave with Becky and their classmates. That same night, Huck sees Injun Joe and his partner making off with a box. He follows and overhears their plans to attack the Widow Douglas, a kind resident of St. Petersburg. By running to fetch help, Huck forestalls the violence and becomes an anonymous hero.

Tom and Becky get lost in the cave, and their absence is not discovered until the following morning. The men of the town begin to search for them, but to no avail. Tom and Becky run out of food and candles and begin to weaken. The horror of the situation increases when Tom, looking for a way out of the cave, happens upon Injun Joe, who is using the cave as a hideout. Eventually, just as the searchers are giving up, Tom finds a way out. The town celebrates, and Becky's father, Judge Thatcher, locks up the cave. Injun Joe, trapped inside, starves to death.

A week later, Tom takes Huck to the cave and they find the box of gold, the proceeds of which are invested for them. The Widow Douglas adopts Huck, and, when Huck attempts to escape civilized life, Tom promises him that if he returns to the widow, he can join Tom's robber band. Reluctantly, Huck agrees.

Character List

Tom Sawyer The novel's protagonist. Tom is a mischievous boy with an active imagination who spends most of the novel getting himself, and often his friends, into and out of trouble. Despite his mischief, Tom has a good heart and a strong moral conscience. As the novel progresses, he begins to take more seriously the responsibilities of his role as a leader among his schoolfellows.

Aunt Polly Tom's aunt and guardian. Aunt Polly is a simple, kindhearted woman who struggles to balance her love for her nephew with her duty to discipline him. She generally fails in her attempts to keep Tom under control because, although she worries about Tom's safety, she seems to fear constraining him too much. Above all, Aunt Polly wants to be appreciated and loved.

Huckleberry Finn The son of the town drunk. Huck is a juvenile outcast who is shunned by respectable society and adored by the local boys, who envy his freedom. Like Tom, Huck is highly superstitious, and both boys are always ready for an adventure. Huck gradually replaces Tom's friend Joe Harper as Tom's sidekick in his escapades.

Becky Thatcher Judge Thatcher's pretty, yellow-haired daughter. From almost the minute she moves to town, Becky is the "Adored Unknown" who stirs Tom's lively romantic sensibility. Naïve at first, Becky soon matches Tom as a romantic strategist, and the two go to great lengths to make each other jealous.

Joe Harper Tom's "bosom friend" and frequent playmate. Joe is a typical best friend, a convention Twain parodies when he refers to Joe and Tom as "two souls with but a single thought." Though Joe mostly mirrors Tom, he diverges from Tom's example when he is the first of the boys to succumb to homesickness on Jackson's Island. As the novel progresses, Huck begins to assume Joe's place as Tom's companion.

Sid Tom's half-brother. Sid is a goody-goody who enjoys getting Tom into trouble. He is mean-spirited but presents a superficial show of model behavior. He is thus the opposite of Tom, who is warmhearted but behaves badly.

Mary Tom's sweet, almost saintly cousin. Mary holds a soft spot for Tom. Like Sid, she is well behaved, but unlike him, she acts out of genuine affection rather than malice.

Injun Joe A violent, villainous man who commits murder, becomes a robber, and plans to mutilate the Widow Douglas. Injun Joe's predominant motivation is revenge. Half Native American and half Caucasian, he has suffered social exclusion, probably because of his race.

Muff Potter A hapless drunk and friend of Injun Joe. Potter is kind and grateful toward Tom and Huck, who bring him presents after he is wrongly jailed for Dr. Robinson's murder. Potter's naïve trust eventually pushes Tom's conscience to the breaking point, compelling Tom to tell the truth at Potter's trial about who actually committed the murder.

Dr. Robinson A respected local physician. Dr. Robinson shows his more sordid side on the night of his murder: he hires Injun Joe and Muff Potter to dig up Hoss Williams's grave because he wants to use the corpse for medical experiments.

Mr. Sprague The minister of the town church.

The Widow Douglas A kindhearted, pious resident of St. Petersburg whom the children recognize as a friend. Tom knows that the Widow Douglas will give him and Becky ice cream and let them sleep over. She is kind to Huck even before she learns that he saved her life.

Mr. Jones A Welshman who lives with his sons near the Widow Douglas's house. Mr. Jones responds to Huck's alarm on the night that Injun Joe intends to attack the widow, and he takes care of Huck in the aftermath.

Judge Thatcher Becky's father, the county judge. A local celebrity, Judge Thatcher inspires the respect of all the townspeople. He takes responsibility for issues affecting the community as a whole, such as closing the cave for safety reasons and taking charge of the boys' treasure money.

Jim Aunt Polly's young slave.

Amy Lawrence Tom's former love. Tom abandons Amy when Becky Thatcher comes to town.

Ben Rogers One of Tom's friends, whom Tom persuades to whitewash Aunt Polly's fence.

Alfred Temple A well-dressed new boy in town. Like Amy Lawrence, Alfred gets caught in the crossfire of Tom and Becky's love games, as Becky pretends to like him in order to make Tom jealous.

Mr. Walters The somewhat ridiculous Sunday school superintendent. Because he aspires to please Judge Thatcher, Mr. Walters rewards Tom with a Bible, even though he knows that Tom hasn't earned it.

Mr. Dobbins The schoolmaster. Mr. Dobbins seems a slightly sad character: his ambition to be a medical doctor has been thwarted and he has become a heavy drinker and the butt of schoolboy pranks.

ANALYSIS OF MAJOR CHARACTERS

TOM SAWYER

When the novel begins, Tom is a mischievous child who envies Huck Finn's lazy lifestyle and freedom. As Tom's adventures proceed, however, critical moments show Tom moving away from his childhood concerns and making mature, responsible decisions. These moments include Tom's testimony at Muff Potter's trial, his saving of Becky from punishment, and his heroic navigation out of the cave. By the end of the novel, Tom is coaxing Huck into staying at the Widow Douglas's, urging his friend to accept tight collars, Sunday school, and good table manners. He is no longer a disobedient character undermining the adult order, but a defender of respectability and responsibility. In the end, growing up for Tom means embracing social custom and sacrificing the freedoms of childhood.

Yet Tom's development isn't totally coherent. The novel jumps back and forth among several narrative strands: Tom's general misbehavior, which climaxes in the Jackson's Island adventure; his courtship of Becky, which culminates in his acceptance of blame for the book that she rips; and his struggle with Injun Joe, which ends with Tom and Huck's discovery of the treasure. Because of the picaresque, or episodic, nature of the plot, Tom's character can seem inconsistent, as it varies depending upon his situation. Tom is a paradoxical figure in some respects—for example, he has no determinate age. Sometimes Tom shows the naïveté of a smaller child, with his interest in make-believe and superstitions. On the other hand, Tom's romantic interest in Becky and his fascination with Huck's smoking and drinking seem more the concerns of an adolescent.

Whether or not a single course of development characterizes Tom's adventures, a single character trait—Tom's unflagging energy and thirst for adventure—propels the novel from episode to episode. Disobedient though he may be, Tom ends up as St. Petersburg's hero. As the town gossips say, "[Tom] would be President, yet, if he escaped hanging."

HUCKLEBERRY FINN

In Huckleberry Finn, Mark Twain created a character who exemplifies freedom within, and from, American society. Huck lives on the margins of society because, as the son of the town drunk, he is pretty much an orphan. He sleeps where he pleases, provided that nobody chases him off, and he eats when he pleases, provided that he can find a morsel. No one requires him to attend school or church, bathe, or dress respectably. It is understandable, if not expected, that Huck smokes and swears. Years of having to fend for himself have invested Huck with a solid common sense and a practical competence that complement Tom's dreamy idealism and fantastical approach to reality (Tom creates worlds for himself that are based on those in stories he has read). But Huck does have two traits in common with Tom: a zest for adventure and a belief in superstition.

Through Huck, Twain weighs the costs and benefits of living in a society against those of living independently of society. For most of the novel, adult society disapproves of Huck, but because Twain renders Huck such a likable boy, the adults' disapproval of Huck generally alienates us from them and not from Huck himself. After Huck saves the Widow Douglas and gets rich, the scale tips in the direction of living in society. But Huck, unlike Tom, isn't convinced that the exchange of freedom for stability is worth it. He has little use for the money he has found and is quite devoted to his rough, independent lifestyle. When the novel ends, Huck, like Tom, is still a work in progress, and we aren't sure whether the Widow Douglas's attempts to civilize him will succeed (Twain reserves the conclusion of Huck's story for his later novel, *The Adventures of Huckleberry Finn*).

INJUN JOE

Injun Joe is *Tom Sawyer*'s villain. His actions are motivated, from beginning to end, by unadulterated malevolence. When Injun Joe explains his motivation for revenge against Dr. Robinson and later against the Widow Douglas, we see that his personal history involves others mistreating and excluding him. Yet the disproportion between the wrongs Injun Joe has suffered—at least as he enumerates them—and the level of vengeance he hopes to exact is so extreme that we aren't tempted to excuse his behavior. In contrast, Muff Potter's misdeeds are inconsequential compared to the punishment he stands to receive. One might also compare Injun Joe to Sid: both are motivated by malice, which they paper over with a convincing performance of innocence.

Though his appearance changes when he disguises himself as a deaf and mute Spaniard, Injun Joe undergoes no real character development over the course of the novel. He never seems to repent for his crimes or change his spiteful outlook. His reappearances in different parts of the novel help to provide a thread of continuity, as they bring the murder-case plot, the treasure-hunt plot, and the adventures-in-the-cave plots together into a single narrative. Injun Joe's presence also adds suspense to the novel, because we have very little sense of whether Tom and Huck's constant fear that Injun Joe will hurt them has any basis in reality.

THEMES, MOTIFS & SYMBOLS

THEMES

Themes are the fundamental and often universal ideas explored in a literary work.

MORAL AND SOCIAL MATURATION

When the novel opens, Tom is engaged in and often the organizer of childhood pranks and make-believe games. As the novel progresses, these initially consequence-free childish games take on more and more gravity. Tom leads himself, Joe Harper, Huck, and, in the cave, Becky Thatcher into increasingly dangerous situations. He also finds himself in predicaments in which he must put his concern for others above his concern for himself, such as when he takes Becky's punishment and when he testifies at Injun Joe's trial. As Tom begins to take initiative to help others instead of himself, he shows his increasing maturity, competence, and moral integrity.

Tom's adventures to Jackson's Island and McDougal's Cave take him away from society. These symbolic removals help to prepare him to return to the village with a new, more adult outlook on his relationship to the community. Though early on Tom looks up to Huck as much older and wiser, by the end of the novel, Tom's maturity has surpassed Huck's. Tom's personal growth is evident in his insistence, in the face of Huck's desire to flee all social constraints, that Huck stay with the Widow Douglas and become civilized.

SOCIETY'S HYPOCRISY

Twain complicates Tom's position on the border between childhood and adulthood by ridiculing and criticizing the values and practices of the adult world toward which Tom is heading. Twain's harshest satire exposes the hypocrisy—and often the essential childishness—of social institutions such as school, church, and the law, as well as public opinion. He also mocks individuals, although when doing so he tends to be less biting and focuses on flaws of character that we understand to be universal.

Twain shows that social authority does not always operate on wise, sound, or consistent principles and that institutions fall prey to the same kinds of mistakes that individuals do. In his depiction of families, Twain shows parental authority and constraint balanced by parental love and indulgence. Though she attempts to restrain and punish Tom, Aunt Polly always relents because of her love for her nephew. As the novel proceeds, a similar tendency toward indulgence becomes apparent within the broader community as well. The community shows its indulgence when Tom's dangerous adventures provoke an outpouring of concern: the community is perfectly ready to forgive Tom's wrongs if it can be sure of his safety. Twain ridicules the ability of this collective tendency toward generosity and forgiveness to go overboard when he describes the town's sentimental forgiveness of the villainous Injun Joe after his death.

The games the children play often seem like attempts to subvert authority and escape from conventional society. Skipping school, sneaking out at night, playing tricks on the teacher, and running away for days at a time are all ways of breaking the rules and defying authority. Yet, Twain shows us that these games can be more conventional than they seem. Tom is highly concerned with conforming to the codes of behavior that he has learned from reading, and he outlines the various criteria that define a pirate, a Robin Hood, or a circus clown. The boys' obsession with superstition is likewise an addiction to convention, which also mirrors the adult society's focus on religion. Thus, the novel shows that adult existence is more similar to childhood existence than it might seem. Though the novel is critical of society's hypocrisy—that is, of the frequent discord between its values and its behavior—Twain doesn't really advocate subversion. The novel demonstrates the potential dangers of subverting authority just as it demonstrates the dangers of adhering to authority too strictly.

FREEDOM THROUGH SOCIAL EXCLUSION

St. Petersburg is an insular community in which outsiders are easily identified. The most notable local outsiders include Huck Finn, who fends for himself outside of any family structure because his father is a drunkard; Muff Potter, also a drunk; and Injun Joe, a malevolent half-breed. Despite the community's clear separation of outsiders from insiders, however, it seems to have a strong impulse toward inclusiveness. The community tolerates the drunkenness of a harmless rascal like Muff Potter, and Huck is more or less protected even though he exists on the fringes of society. Tom too is an orphan who has been taken in by Aunt Polly out of love and filial responsibility. Injun Joe is the only resident of St. Petersburg who is completely excluded from the community. Only after Injun Joe's death are the townspeople able to transform him, through their manipulation of his memory, into a tolerable part of St. Petersburg society.

Huck's exclusion means that many of the other children are not allowed to play with him. He receives no structured education and often does not even have enough to eat or a place to sleep. Twain minimizes these concerns, however, in favor of presenting the freedom that Huck's low social status affords him. Huck can smoke and sleep outside and do all the things that the other boys dream of doing, with very little constraint. Huck's windfall at the end of the novel, when the boys find the treasure, threatens to stifle his freedom. The Widow Douglas's attentions force Huck to change his lifestyle, something Huck would probably never choose to do on his own. By linking Huck's acquisition of the treasure with his assimilation into St. Petersburg society, Twain emphasizes the association between financial standing and social standing. Besides the obvious fact that money is an important ingredient in social acceptance, social existence clearly is itself a kind of economy, in which certain costs accompany certain benefits. The price of social inclusion is a loss of complete freedom.

Superstition in an Uncertain World

Twain first explores superstition in the graveyard, where Tom and Huck go to try out a magical cure for warts. From this point forward, superstition becomes an important element in all of the boys' decision-making. The convenient aspect of Tom and Huck's superstitious beliefs is that there are so many of them, and they are so freely interpretable; Tom and Huck can pick and choose whichever belief suits their needs at the time. In this regard, Twain suggests, superstition bears a resemblance to religion—at least as the populace of St. Petersburg practices it.

The humorousness of the boys' obsession with witches, ghosts, and graveyards papers over, to some extent, the real horror of the circumstances to which the boys are exposed: grave digging, murder, starvation, and attempted mutilation. The relative ease with which they assimilate these ghastly events into their childish world is perhaps one of the least realistic aspects of the novel. (If the novel were written today, we might expect to read about the psychic damage these extreme childhood experiences have done to these boys.) The boys negotiate all this horror because they exist in a world suspended somewhere between reality and make-believe. Their fear of death is real and pervasive, for example, but we also have the sense that they do not really understand death and all of its ramifications.

MOTIFS

Motifs are recurring structures, contrasts, and literary devices that can help to develop and inform the text's major themes.

CRIME
The many crimes committed in the novel range from minor childhood transgressions to capital offenses—from playing hooky to murder. The games the boys prefer center on crime as well, giving them a chance to explore the boldness and heroism involved in breaking social expectations without actually threatening the social order. The boys want to be pirates, robbers, and murderers even though they feel remorse when they actually commit the minor crime of stealing bacon. The two scenes in which Tom plays Robin Hood—who, in stealing from the rich and giving to the poor is both a criminal and a hero—are emblematic of how Tom associates crime with defending values and even altering the structure of society.

TRADING
The children in the novel maintain an elaborate miniature economy in which they constantly trade amongst themselves treasures that would be junk to adults. These exchanges replicate the commercial relationships in which the children will have to engage when they get older. Many of the complications that money creates appear in their exchanges. Tom swindles his friends out of all their favorite objects through a kind of false advertising when he sells them the opportunity to whitewash the fence. He then uses his newly acquired wealth to buy power and prestige at Sunday school—rewards that should be earned rather than bought. When Tom and Joe fight over the tick in class, we see a case in which a disagreement leads the boys, who have been sharing quite civilly, to revert to a quarrel over ownership.

The jump from this small-scale property holding at the beginning of the novel to the $12,000 treasure at the end is an extreme one. In spite of all Tom and Huck's practice, their money is given to a responsible adult. With their healthy allowance, the boys can continue to explore their role as commercial citizens, but at a more moderate rate.

THE CIRCUS

The boys mention again and again their admiration for the circus life and their desire to be clowns when they grow up. These references emphasize the innocence with which they approach the world. Rather than evaluate the real merits and shortcomings of the various occupations Tom and Hank could realistically choose, they like to imagine themselves in roles they find romantic or exciting.

SHOWING OFF

Tom's showing off is mostly directed toward Becky Thatcher. When he shows off initially, we guess that he literally prances around and does gymnastics. Later, the means by which Tom and Becky try to impress each other grow more subtle, as they manipulate Amy and Alfred in an effort to make each other jealous.

In the Sunday school scene, Twain reveals that showing off is not strictly a childhood practice. The adults who are supposed to be authority figures in the church are so awed by Judge Thatcher and so eager to attract his attention and approval that they too begin to behave like children. The room devolves into an absolute spectacle of ridiculous behavior by children and adults alike, culminating in the public embarrassment in which Tom exposes his ignorance of the Bible.

SYMBOLS

Symbols are objects, characters, figures, and colors used to represent abstract ideas or concepts.

THE CAVE

The cave represents a trial that Tom has to pass before he can graduate into maturity. Coming-of-age stories often involve tests in which the protagonist is separated from the rest of the society for a period of time and faces significant dangers or challenges. Only after having survived on the strength of his personal resources is Tom ready to rejoin society.

SYMBOLS

THE STORM

The storm on Jackson's Island symbolizes the danger involved in the boys' removal from society. It forms part of an interruptive pattern in the novel, in which periods of relative peace and tranquility alternate with episodes of high adventure or danger. Later, when Tom is sick, he believes that the storm hit to indicate that God's wrath is directed at him personally. The storm thus becomes an external symbol of Tom's conscience.

THE TREASURE

The treasure is a symbolic goal that marks the end of the boys' journey. It becomes a indicator of Tom's transition into adulthood and Huck's movement into civilized society. It also symbolizes the boys' heroism, marking them as exceptional in a world where conformity is the rule.

THE VILLAGE

Many readers interpret the small village of St. Petersburg as a microcosm of the United States or of society in general. All of the major social institutions are present on a small scale in the village and all are susceptible to Twain's comic treatment. The challenges and joys Tom encounters in the village are, in their basic structure, ones that he or any reader could expect to meet anywhere.

Summary & Analysis

Chapters 1–3

Summary—Chapter 1: Tom Plays, Fights, and Hides

*Spare the rod and spile the child, as the Good Book
says. I'm a-laying up sin and suffering for us both, I
know. He's full of the Old Scratch, but laws-a-me! he's
my own dead sister's boy, poor thing, and I ain't got
the heart to lash him, somehow.*

(See QUOTATIONS, p. 53)

The novel opens with Aunt Polly scouring the house in search of her
nephew, Tom Sawyer. She finds him in the closet, discovers that his
hands are covered with jam, and prepares to give him a whipping.
Tom cries out theatrically, "Look behind you!" and when Aunt
Polly turns, Tom escapes over the fence. After Tom is gone, Aunt
Polly reflects ruefully on Tom's mischief and how she lets him get
away with too much.

Tom comes home at suppertime to help Aunt Polly's young slave,
Jim, chop wood. Tom also wants to tell Jim about his adventures.
During supper, Aunt Polly asks Tom leading questions in an attempt
to confirm her suspicion that he skipped school that afternoon and
went swimming instead. Tom explains his wet hair by saying that
he pumped water on his head and shows her that his collar is still
sewn from the morning, which means that he couldn't have taken
his shirt off to swim. Aunt Polly is satisfied, but Sid, Tom's half-
brother, points out that the shirt thread, which was white in the
morning, is now black. Tom has resewn the shirt himself to disguise
his delinquency.

Tom goes out of the house furious with Sid, but he soon forgets
his anger as he practices a new kind of whistling. While wandering
the streets of St. Petersburg, his town, he encounters a newcomer, a
boy his own age who appears overdressed and arrogant. Tom and
the new arrival exchange insults for a while and then begin wrestling. Tom overcomes his antagonist and eventually chases the newcomer all the way home.

When he returns home in the evening, Tom finds Aunt Polly waiting for him. She notices his dirtied clothes and resolves to make him work the next day, a Saturday, as punishment.

SUMMARY—CHAPTER 2: THE GLORIOUS WHITEWASHER

> *"Say, Tom, let me whitewash a little."*
> (See QUOTATIONS, p. 54)

On Saturday morning, Aunt Polly sends Tom out to whitewash the fence. Jim passes by, and Tom tries to get him to do some of the whitewashing in return for a "white alley," a kind of marble. Jim almost agrees, but Aunt Polly appears and chases him off, leaving Tom alone with his labor.

A little while later, Ben Rogers, another boy Tom's age, walks by. Tom convinces Ben that whitewashing a fence is great pleasure, and after some bargaining, Ben agrees to give Tom his apple in exchange for the privilege of working on the fence. Over the course of the day, every boy who passes ends up staying to whitewash, and each one gives Tom something in exchange. By the time the fence has three coats, Tom has collected a hoard of miscellaneous treasures. Tom muses that all it takes to make someone want something is to make that thing hard to get.

SUMMARY—CHAPTER 3: BUSY AT WAR AND LOVE

Aunt Polly is pleasantly surprised to find the work done, and she allows Tom to go out in the late afternoon. On his way, he pelts Sid with clods of dirt in revenge for his treachery in the matter of the shirt collar. He then hastens to the town square, where a group of boys are fighting a mock battle. Tom and his friend Joe Harper act as generals. Tom's army wins the battle.

On his way home for dinner, Tom passes the Thatcher house and catches sight of a beautiful girl. He falls head over heels in love with her. Quickly forgetting his last love, a girl named Amy Lawrence, Tom spends the rest of the afternoon "showing off" on the street. The girl tosses him a flower, and, after some more showing off, Tom reluctantly returns home.

At dinner, Sid breaks the sugar bowl, and Tom is blamed. Tom's mood changes, and he wanders out after dinner feeling mistreated and melodramatic, imagining how sorry Aunt Polly would be if he turned up dead. Eventually, he finds his way back to the beautiful girl's house and prepares to die pitifully beneath her window. Just then, a maid opens the window and dumps a pitcher of water on his head. Tom scurries home and goes to bed as Sid watches in silence.

ANALYSIS — CHAPTERS 1–3

The first word of the novel—Aunt Polly's shout of "TOM!"—immediately establishes Aunt Polly's role as disciplinarian and Tom's role as troublemaker. Tom and Aunt Polly's initial confrontation quickly characterizes Tom as clever enough to escape punishment and Aunt Polly as someone who threatens harsh discipline but who, for all her bluster, is really quite fond of her nephew. "Every time I hit him," she says, "my old heart most breaks." Aunt Polly knows that she must discipline Tom in order to help him mature successfully into responsible adulthood, but there is a part of her that balks at impinging on the freedom of such a creative and headstrong child. That the softhearted Aunt Polly is Tom's only authority figure in the home explains Tom's relatively large degree of freedom. Huckleberry Finn, the son of the town drunk, offers an even more extreme example of a child who lives outside of the normal structures of authority, whether parental, social, or legal.

By depicting the fighting, playing, and trading in which the children engage as elaborate rituals, Twain emphasizes that the world of childhood is governed by its own social rules, which serve as a kind of practice for, and microcosm of, adulthood. The reality of the surrounding adult social world manifests itself in the brief appearance of the slave boy, Jim, abruptly reminding us that the novel is set in the slaveholding South. Unlike Twain's later novel *Huckleberry Finn*, however, slavery and criticism of slavery exist in *Tom Sawyer* only in the background; Tom's idyllic childhood adventures remain the novel's focus.

The scene in which Tom persuades his peers to do all his whitewashing work establishes Tom's position as a leader among his peers and as an initiative-taking mastermind. Though a troublemaker, Tom at times presents a hint of maturity that his comrades lack. Joe Harper, Tom's friend who acts as the opposing general in the mock battle, serves as a sidekick throughout the novel, mostly following Tom's lead. Because of his comparatively dull nature and flat characterization, Joe highlights Tom's vibrancy. Sid, Tom's halfbrother, is presented as Tom's opposite—whereas Tom is a mischiefmaker with a noble heart, Sid is a well-behaved child whose heart is basically evil.

Tom's pursuit of his "Adored Unknown" (we find out later that the girl's name is Becky Thatcher) also helps to pinpoint his level of maturity. The fact that he is interested in a girl shows him to be mature compared to his friends, but his "showing off" for Becky, along with his melodramatic desire to die under her window after Aunt Polly falsely blames him for breaking the sugar bowl, spring from the sensitivity and sensibility of a young boy. Furthermore, the fluidity of Tom's imagination—he moves with ease from one game or occupation to the next—testifies to his youthful manner of experiencing the world.

CHAPTERS 4–6

SUMMARY—CHAPTER 4: SHOWING OFF IN SUNDAY SCHOOL

> *Mr. Walters fell to "showing off," with all sorts of official bustlings and activities. . . . The librarian "showed off". . . . The young lady teachers "showed off". . . . The little girls "showed off" in various ways, and the little boys "showed off."*
>
> *(See* QUOTATIONS, *p. 55)*

Sunday morning arrives, and Tom prepares for Sunday school with the help of his cousin Mary. As Tom struggles halfheartedly to learn his Bible verses, Mary encourages and entices him with the promise of "something ever so nice." Tom's work ethic then improves, and he manages to memorize the verses. Mary gives him a "Barlow" knife as reward. Tom then dresses for church, and he, Mary, and Sid hurry off to Sunday school, which Tom loathes.

Before class begins, Tom trades all the spoils he has gained from his whitewashing scam for tickets. The tickets are given as rewards for well-recited Bible verses, and a student who has memorized two thousand verses and received the appropriate tickets can trade them in for a copy of the Bible, awarded with honor in front of the entire class.

Judge Thatcher, the uncle of Tom's friend Jeff Thatcher, visits Tom's class that day. The judge's family includes his daughter, Becky—the beautiful girl Tom notices the previous afternoon. The class treats the judge as a celebrity—the students, teachers, and superintendent make a great attempt at showing off for him. As usual, Tom is the best show-off—by trading for tickets before class, Tom has accumulated enough to earn a Bible. Mr. Walters, Tom's

Sunday school teacher, is flabbergasted when Tom approaches with the tickets. He knows that Tom has not memorized the appropriate number of verses, but since Tom has the required tickets, and since Mr. Walters is eager to impress Judge Thatcher, the Bible-awarding ceremony proceeds.

The Judge pats Tom on the head and compliments him on his diligence. He gives him the chance to show off his purported knowledge, asking him, "No doubt you know the names of all the twelve disciples. Won't you tell us the names of the first two that were appointed?" Tom does not know their names, of course, and eventually blurts out the first two names that come to his mind: David and Goliath. The narrator pleads, "Let us draw the curtain of charity over the rest of the scene."

SUMMARY—CHAPTER 5: THE PINCH-BUG AND HIS PREY

After Sunday school comes the church service, which includes a long, tedious sermon. At one point, the minister describes how, at the millennium (the 1,000-year period during which Christ will reign over the earth, according to Christianity) the lion and the lamb will lie down together and a little child shall lead them. Tom wishes that he could be that child—as long as the lion were tame.

Bored, Tom takes from his pocket a box containing a "pinchbug," or a large black beetle. The insect pinches him and slips from his grasp to the middle of the aisle at the same time that a stray poodle wanders into the church. The dog investigates the pinchbug, receives one pinch, circles the insect warily, and then eventually sits on it. The bug latches onto the poodle's behind, and the unfortunate dog runs yelping through the church until its master flings it out a window. The general laughter disrupts the sermon completely, and Tom goes home happy, despite the loss of his bug.

SUMMARY—CHAPTER 6: TOM MEETS BECKY

On Monday morning, Tom feigns a "mortified toe" with the hope of staying home from school. When that ploy fails, he complains of a toothache, but Aunt Polly yanks out the loose tooth and sends him off to school.

On his way to school, Tom encounters Huckleberry Finn, the son of the town drunkard. Huck is "cordially hated and dreaded by all the mothers of the town," who fear that he will be a bad influence on their children. But every boy, including Tom, admires Huck and envies him for his ability to avoid school and work without fear of punishment. Huck and Tom converse, comparing notes on charms to remove warts. Huck carries with him a dead cat, which he plans to take to the graveyard that night. According to superstition, when the devil comes to take the corpse of a wicked person, the dead cat will follow the corpse, and the warts will follow the cat. Tom agrees to go with Huck to the cemetery that night, trades his yanked tooth for a tick from Huck, and continues on to school.

Tom arrives late, and the schoolmaster demands an explanation. Tom notices an open seat on the girls' side of the room, next to Becky Thatcher. He decides to get in trouble on purpose, knowing that he will be sent to sit with the girls as punishment. He boldly declares, "I stopped to talk with Huckleberry Finn!" The horrified teacher whips Tom and sends him to the seat next to Becky.

Tom offers Becky a peach and tries to interest her by drawing a picture on his slate. Becky initially shies from Tom's attentions, but she soon warms to him and promises to stay at school with him during lunch. Becky and Tom introduce themselves, and Tom scrawls "I love you" on his slate. At this point, the teacher collars Tom and drags him back to the boys' side of the room.

ANALYSIS — CHAPTERS 4–6

Twain renders Tom's cousin Mary as an idealized character whose total goodness leads her to forgive the faults of others. Unlike Sid, who behaves well but delights in getting Tom in trouble, Mary behaves well and attempts to keep Tom *out* of mischief. Her motherly caring for Tom is manifest not only in her eagerness for Tom to learn Bible verses but also in her name, which evokes that of Mary, mother of Jesus.

In the Sunday school scenes, Twain gently satirizes the tradition of making children memorize Bible verses. He points out the cheapness of the prize—"a very plainly bound Bible"—and relates the story of a German boy who "had once recited three thousand verses without stopping" and afterward suffered a nervous breakdown. In calling the boy's collapse "a grievous misfortune for the school" (since the school relied on the German boy to perform for guests), Twain implies that the students are memorizing verses not for real spiritual growth but for the sake of making their teachers and superintendent look good. Twain furthers this implication by illustrating Mr. Walters's eagerness to display a "prodigy," or extremely talented youth, for Judge Thatcher.

Twain's critique is compassionate, however. His intention is not to expose anything inherently unworthy in his characters but to point out universal human weaknesses. When Judge Thatcher visits, everyone at Sunday school shows off—the superintendent, librarian, teachers, boys, and girls—in an attempt to attract the local celebrity's attention. Tom arranges to earn an honor he doesn't deserve, teachers dote on students they usually treat severely, and the superintendent gives a reward to a child (Tom) whom he knows doesn't deserve it. By exposing the superficiality of the Sunday school's workings, Twain makes Tom's own dramatic inclinations seem not a departure from, but an exaggeration of, his society's behavior.

As Twain describes the church service in Chapter 5, he again shows Tom's faults replicated in the behavior of adults. Tom is restless and inattentive in the usual childlike manner, but he is not alone—the congregation as a whole drifts toward slumber, and "many a head by and by began to nod." Tom's desire to be the child leading the lion and the lamb, while misguided, demonstrates that he is at least listening to some of the sermon. That the rest of the congregation is so easily distracted supports the idea that Tom's lack of interest in and misunderstanding of the sermon constitute the universal response to the monotonous minister.

By releasing the pinchbug and creating havoc, Tom succeeds in doing what the sermon cannot—he gets the congregation's attention. With more people caring about the pinchbug than about the minister's fire and brimstone, the church service begins to seem as ridiculous as the struggle between the poodle and the insect. Again, however, Twain's satire is not cruel. Nobody is accused of being irreligious or wicked for falling asleep during the service. Rather, Twain exposes the comic and sometimes ridiculous elements of traditions, such as churchgoing, that bind the community together.

In the scene following the church service, we meet Huckleberry Finn, one of the most famous figures in American literature. Huck enjoys what Tom and every other mischievous boy secretly wishes he could attain—complete freedom from adult authority. Unlike Tom, who is parentless but has Aunt Polly to limit his liberty, Huck has no adults controlling him at all. His father is the town drunkard, leaving Huck to wander as he pleases—"everything that goes to make life precious, that boy had." From a boy's perspective, Huck can do all the important things—swimming, playing, cursing, fishing, walking barefoot—without enduring the burdens of church, school, personal hygiene, or parental harassment.

Given Tom's inability to keep his mind from wandering during the church sermon, Huck and Tom's earnest enthusiasm for superstition in their conversation about the causes of warts is particularly notable. Tom may not be interested in memorizing Bible verses, but he and his companions are fascinated by the intricate details of charms, magical cures, and other varieties of folk wisdom. The boys' unwavering belief in the efficacy of the wart cures resembles religious fervor in its dependence upon explanations that exist outside the bounds of human understanding. They want so strongly to believe in the supernatural that when a charm seems not to work, they are quick to furnish what they consider a rational explanation for its failure rather than concede that their charms don't work at all.

Chapters 7–10

SUMMARY—CHAPTER 7: TICK-RUNNING AND A HEARTBREAK

The teacher now places Tom next to Joe Harper. After trying to study for a while, Tom gives up and he and Joe play with the tick, each attempting to keep the bug on his side of the desk by harassing it with a pin. They begin arguing midway through the game, and the teacher again appears behind Tom, this time to deliver a tremendous whack to both boys.

During lunch, Tom and Becky sit in the empty schoolroom together, and Tom persuades her to "get engaged" to him—an agreement they render solemn by saying "I love you" and kissing. Tom begins talking excitedly about how much he enjoys being engaged and accidentally reveals that he was previously engaged to Amy Lawrence. Becky begins to cry and says that Tom must still love Amy. Tom denies it, swearing that he loves only Becky, but she cries harder and refuses to accept the brass andiron knob he offers her as a token of his affection. When Tom marches out, Becky realizes that he won't return that day and becomes even more upset.

SUMMARY—CHAPTER 8: A PIRATE BOLD TO BE

For the rest of the afternoon, Tom wanders about in a forest, first deciding that he will become a pirate, next trying a futile charm to locate his lost marbles, and finally encountering Joe Harper. The boys play Robin Hood and then go home, in agreement that "they would rather be outlaws a year in Sherwood Forest than President of the United States forever."

SUMMARY — CHAPTER 9: TRAGEDY IN THE GRAVEYARD

That night, Tom sneaks out of bed and goes to the graveyard with Huck. They hide in a clump of elms a few feet from the fresh grave of Hoss Williams and wait for devils to appear. After a while, three figures approach the grave. The boys believe with horrified delight that these are the devils, but they turn out to be three adults from the town carrying out a midnight mission of their own. Tom and Huck are surprised to discover the young Dr. Robinson accompanied by two local outcasts, the drunken Muff Potter and Injun Joe.

Dr. Robinson orders the other two men to dig up Hoss Williams's corpse, presumably for use in medical experiments. After they finish the job, Potter demands extra payment, and Robinson refuses. Injun Joe then reminds Robinson of an incident that happened five years earlier, when Injun Joe came begging at the Robinsons' kitchen door and was turned away. Injun Joe now intends to have his revenge. A fight ensues; Dr. Robinson knocks Injun Joe down and then is attacked by Potter. He uses Hoss Williams's headstone to defend himself, knocking Potter unconscious. In the scuffle, Injun Joe stabs Dr. Robinson with Potter's knife.

The terrified boys flee without being detected by the men. Eventually, Potter awakens and asks Injun Joe what happened. Injun Joe tells the drunk Potter that Potter murdered Dr. Robinson in a drunken fury, and Potter, still dazed, believes him. Injun Joe promises not to tell anyone about the crime, and they part ways. Before Injun Joe leaves the graveyard, however, he notes smugly that Potter's knife remains stuck in the corpse.

SUMMARY — CHAPTER 10: DIRE PROPHECY OF
THE HOWLING DOG

The boys run to a deserted tannery and hide, unaware of Injun Joe's plot to blame Potter for the murder. They decide that if they tell what they saw and Injun Joe escapes hanging, he will probably kill them. Consequently, they decide to swear in blood never to tell anyone what they saw. After taking the oath, they hear the howls of a stray dog, which they interpret as a sign that whomever the animal is howling at will die. Tom and Huck assume the dog's howls are for them, but when they go outside, they see that the dog is facing Muff Potter.

Tom goes home and crawls into bed. Sid, still awake, takes note of Tom's late arrival and tells Aunt Polly about it the next morning. She lectures Tom and asks how he can go on breaking her heart;

her heavy sorrow is for Tom a punishment "worse than a thousand whippings." Tom goes off to school dejected. On his desk he finds the brass andiron knob he tried to give to Becky the day before, and his anguish deepens.

ANALYSIS — CHAPTERS 7–10

As his Robin Hood game shows, Tom assimilates and adheres to the conventions of the heroic and romantic stories in which he is so steeped. He memorizes situations and even exact dialogue from these stories in order to re-create them in his own games. Tom's courtship of Becky also follows the conventions of romantic literature, albeit in a somewhat adulterated form.

With the ability to memorize and re-create situations according to stories and literature, Tom shows that he has highly developed mental skills. Yet, in his conduct and interaction with others, Tom is still immature. This imbalance is evident when Tom accidentally reveals his previous engagement to Amy Lawrence and only watches, unsure of how to act, when Becky cries. His subsequent depression and decision to become a pirate manifest his preference for the youthful world of make-believe and literature over that of real-life relationships. Tom's actions at this point also foreshadow his later adventures with Huck and Joe on Jackson's Island.

The graveyard scene constitutes a turning point in the plot, as it is the first of Tom's adventures that has any moral significance. Up to this point, Tom's adventures have been playful and innocent. As Tom and Huck witness Dr. Robinson's murder, the sordid adult world imposes itself upon their childhood innocence. When they see the figures approaching the grave, both boys assume them to be devils, among the most terrifying things they can envision. Ironically, the presumed devils turn out to be real men who become more frightening than any childhood superstition or imagined vision.

After witnessing the crime, Tom and Huck's immediate inclination is to flee, both physically and symbolically. They run from the scene of the crime back into their world of childhood games by signing a "blood oath" to keep what they have seen a secret. Knowing nothing about Injun Joe's plan to blame hapless Muff Potter for the crime, Huck and Tom assume that Injun Joe will either be caught or will escape. They are understandably afraid of what these wicked men might do to them if they find out that the boys were present at the scene of the crime. As we later see, however, even after Potter is falsely accused and arrested, Tom and Huck are unable to overcome their fears and tell the authorities what they have seen. Instead, their belief in superstition, their adherence to the blood oath, and their assumption that God will strike down Injun Joe for wickedly lying guide their actions. Even though the boys fear Injun Joe, they also fear superstition and, ultimately, God or a higher force that they hope will cancel out the more immediate threat from the murderous Injun Joe.

CHAPTERS 11–13

SUMMARY — CHAPTER 11: CONSCIENCE RACKS TOM
The day after Tom and Huck witness Dr. Robinson's murder, some townspeople discover the doctor's corpse in the graveyard, along with Potter's knife. A crowd gathers in the cemetery, and then Potter himself appears. To Tom, Huck, and especially Potter's shock, Injun Joe describes how Potter committed the crime. Consequently, the sheriff arrests Potter for murder.

Tom's pangs of conscience over not telling the truth about the murder keep him up at night, but Aunt Polly assumes that just hearing about the horrid crime has upset him. Tom begins sneaking to the window of Potter's jail cell every few days to bring him small gifts.

SUMMARY — CHAPTER 12: THE CAT AND THE PAIN-KILLER
Becky Thatcher falls ill and stops coming to school. Tom's depression worsens, so much so that Aunt Polly begins to worry about his health. She gives him various ineffective "treatments," which culminate in an awful-tasting serum called "Pain-killer." Tom finds this last treatment so intolerable that he feeds it to the cat, which reacts with extreme hyperactivity. Aunt Polly discovers what Tom has done, but she begins to realize that "what was cruelty to a cat *might* be cruelty to a boy, too," and sends him off to school without punishment. Becky finally returns to school that morning, but she spurns Tom completely.

SUMMARY — CHAPTER 13: THE PIRATE CREW SET SAIL
Feeling mistreated, Tom resolves to act on his earlier impulse to become a pirate. He meets Joe Harper, who is likewise disaffected because his mother has wrongly accused and punished him for stealing cream. They find Huck Finn, always up for a new adventure, and the three agree to slip away to Jackson's Island, an uninhabited, forested isle three miles downriver from St. Petersburg.

That night, the three boys take a raft and pole their way to the island, calling out meaningless nautical commands to one another as they go. At about two in the morning they arrive on the island, build a fire, and eat some bacon that Joe has stolen for them. For the rest of the night they sit around and discuss pirate conduct. Eventually, however, they think about the meat they stole and reflect on the shamefulness of their petty crime—after all, the Bible explicitly forbids stealing. They decide that "their piracies should not again be sullied with the crime of stealing" and fall asleep.

ANALYSIS—CHAPTERS 11–13

Twain discourages us from feeling sympathy for Injun Joe, the novel's most pronounced villain. We learn that Dr. Robinson once mistreated Injun Joe by chasing him off when he came begging one night, but Injun Joe's willingness to murder a man as retribution for this relatively minor offense and his decision to pin the crime on a pathetic drunk who instinctively trusts him confound our ability to feel sorry for him.

Joe's status as a "half-breed" (he is half "Injun," or Native American, and half white) makes him an outsider in the St. Petersburg community. The novel contains racist suggestions linking Injun Joe's villainy to the presumed contamination of his white blood. Joe tells Dr. Robinson, "The Injun blood ain't in me for nothing," suggesting that the alien, "Injun" part of Joe is what inspires his evil. When Injun Joe reappears in disguise later in the novel, he comes dressed as a deaf and mute Spaniard. In a way, Joe's choice of disguise is logical, given his dark features, but the outfit also reinforces Injun Joe's foreignness.

As in Chapter 8, Becky's rejection turns Tom to thoughts of piracy. Twain mocks the convention in adult romances that unrequited love drives men to desperate acts. Only Huck, who joins Joe Harper and Tom as they act on Tom's pirate fantasy, adds an authentic outlaw element to the adventure. Huck smokes and is something of an outsider in St. Petersburg society. However, whereas Injun Joe is completely ostracized by the St. Petersburg community, Huck Finn is allowed some mobility within it, as Huck's roles—as Tom's companion and, later, as the Widow Douglas's adoptee—show.

The boys' trip to the island and their plans for a pirate career demonstrate their imaginative energy and their innocence. Through several exchanges, the three reveal that they know very little about what being a pirate actually entails. The children's books they have read furnish their entire conception of an outlaw's life. Tom's remarks about pirates that "they have just a bully time ... [they] take ships, and burn them, and get the money and bury it in awful places [but] they don't kill the women—they're too noble" demonstrate the degree to which Tom idealizes these figures. Furthermore, the boys' remorse over the stolen bacon—an actual, and comparatively small, offense—shows that they don't see the storybook misdeeds they venerate as actual sins or punishable offenses. In their shame at having stolen the bacon, they defer to the Ten Commandments and to their own consciences, irrationally deciding that such mean behavior is unworthy of their idealized image of a pirate. Up to this moment, we have seen Tom maturing mentally, as he dreams up scheme after scheme. He has matured through his eye-opening experiences, such as his witness of Dr. Robinson's murder, and he has matured emotionally, as he falls for and is rejected by Becky Thatcher. Tom's rejection of sinful behavior, however, marks the first instance of his moral maturation. We know he has the capacity to memorize and imagine a whole new world of pirates on the high seas, but now we see that he understands right versus wrong as well.

CHAPTERS 14–17

SUMMARY—CHAPTER 14: HAPPY CAMP OF THE FREEBOOTERS
The next day, the boys wake on Jackson's Island and find that their raft has disappeared, but the discovery hardly bothers them. In fact, they find relief in being severed from their last link to St. Petersburg. Huck finds a spring nearby, and the boys go fishing and come up with a bountiful and delicious catch. After breakfast, Tom and Joe explore the island and find pirate life nearly perfect. In the afternoon, however, their enthusiasm and conversation fade, and they begin to feel the first stirrings of homesickness.

In the late afternoon, a large group of boats appears on the river, and, after some confusion, the boys realize that the townspeople are searching for them, assuming they have drowned. This realization actually raises the boys' spirits and makes them feel, temporarily, like heroes. After dinner, however, both Tom and Joe begin to consider the people who may be missing them terribly. Hesitantly, Joe suggests the possibility of returning home, but Tom dismisses the suggestion. That night, however, Tom decides to cross the river back to town to observe the local reaction to their absence. Before he leaves, he writes messages on two sycamore scrolls, then puts one in his pocket and one in Joe's hat.

SUMMARY — CHAPTER 15: TOM'S STEALTHY VISIT HOME

Tom swims from the end of a sandbar to the nearby Illinois shore and stows away on a ferry to cross back to the Missouri side. At home, Tom finds Aunt Polly, Sid, Mary, and Mrs. Harper sitting together. He hides under a bed and listens to their conversation. With the exception of Sid, they all talk about how much they miss the boys and wish they had been kinder to them. Tom learns that the search crew has found the raft downstream, so everyone assumes that the boys capsized in midstream and drowned.

After the company has gone to bed, Tom goes to his aunt's bedside and almost places one of his sycamore scrolls on her table, but he decides against it. He returns to the island, finds Huck and Joe making breakfast, and tells them of his adventures.

SUMMARY — CHAPTER 16: FIRS PIPES — "I'VE LOST MY KNIFE"

The boys find turtle eggs on the sandbar that afternoon and eat fried eggs for supper that night and for breakfast the following morning. They strip naked, swim, and have wrestling matches and a mock circus on the beach. Homesickness mounts, however, and Tom finds himself writing "BECKY" in the sand. Joe suggests again that they return home, and this time Huck sides with him. The two boys prepare to cross the river, and Tom, feeling suddenly lonely and desperate, calls to them to stop. He then tells them of a secret plan that he has devised. After hearing his plan (we do not yet know what it entails), both boys agree to stay and their spirits are rejuvenated.

That afternoon, Tom and Joe ask Huck to teach them how to smoke. Huck makes them pipes, and they sit together smoking and commenting on how easy it is. They imagine the effect they will produce when they go home and smoke casually in front of their friends. Eventually, however, both boys begin to feel sick, drop their pipes, and declare that they need to go look for Joe's knife. Huck finds them later, fast asleep in separate parts of the forest, probably after having vomited. That evening, Huck takes out his pipe and offers to prepare theirs for them, but both boys say they feel too sick—because of something they ate, they claim.

That night, a terrible thunderstorm hits the island. The boys take refuge in their tent, but the wind carries its roof off, so they have to take shelter under a giant oak by the riverbank. They watch in terror as the wind and lightning tear the island apart. When the storm passes, they return to their camp and find that the tree that had sheltered their tent has been completely destroyed.

The boys rebuild their fire out of the embers of the burnt tree and roast some ham. After sleeping for a time, they awaken midmorning and fight their homesickness by pretending to be Indians. At meal-time, however, they realize that Indians cannot eat together without smoking the peace pipe, and so Tom and Joe make a second effort at smoking. This time, they don't become nearly as ill.

SUMMARY — CHAPTER 17: PIRATES AT THEIR OWN FUNERAL

Back in the village, everyone remains in deep mourning. Becky Thatcher regrets her coldness toward Tom, and their schoolmates remember feeling awful premonitions the last time they saw the boys. The next day, Sunday, everyone gathers for the funeral. The minister gives a flattering sermon about the boys, and the congregation wonders how they could have overlooked the goodness in Tom and Joe. Eventually, the entire church breaks down in tears. At that moment, the three boys, according to Tom's plan, enter through a side door after having listened to their own funeral service.

Joe Harper's family, Aunt Polly, and Mary seize their boys and embrace them, leaving Huck standing alone. Tom complains, "[I]t ain't fair. Somebody's got to be glad to see Huck," and Aunt Polly hugs Huck too, embarrassing him further. The congregation then sings "Old Hundred."

ANALYSIS — CHAPTERS 14–17

At earlier points in the novel, Tom's melodramatic self-pity leads him to wish he were dead so that his persecutors would be miserable and sorry for having treated him so unkindly. By running away, he realizes this fantasy to die temporarily and see the reactions of those he has left behind. Ultimately, instead of being a chance to escape adults, the trip to Jackson's Island is reassurance for Tom and Joe that the adults in their lives still love them and need them.

Twain uses humorous irony to criticize the hypocrisy of adult society, which only perceives the worth of its members once they have passed away. While alive, most of the adults in St. Petersburg fail to recognize the worth of Tom, Huck, and Joe (Aunt Polly is an exception). When the town presumes the children dead, how-ever, it frantically calls out search boats and mourns. With all of their mental maturity, even the adults of the town cannot justify the regret they have for not appreciating the boys more during their lives. Ironically, Tom's understanding of how the town will react to the boys' survival proves that even though he is young and preoccupied with imagination and games, he possesses greater knowledge of human psychology than the town members themselves.

Tom and Joe's desire to smoke a pipe reveals that forbidden activities fascinate Tom and his comrades for the prestige that such activities bring them. Whether in fights, in front of girls, or in the classroom, Tom and his friends are constantly showing off. Such performances are critical parts of Tom's boyhood, because they earn him the respect of his peers and liven up the regular routines of small-town life. It is clear that he and Joe want to learn how to smoke so that they will appear special in the eyes of their friends, not because they expect to enjoy the activity. Tom declares, "I'll come up to you and say, 'Joe, got a pipe? I want a smoke.' . . . And then you'll out with the pipes . . . and then just see 'em look." Indeed, the phrase "just see 'em look" captures the motivation behind many of Tom's activities.

This quotation reveals also that Tom is not only a perpetual performer but also a director. As with his funeral, Tom has planned the scene where his friends see him smoke. He seems to relish getting his actors—whether the neighborhood children whom he cons into whitewashing his fence or the pinch-bug he unleashes on the poodle—to perform the parts he has written for them. Even when Joe and Huck rebel against Tom's authority, wanting to return home in Chapter 16, Tom manages to regain control by sharing his brilliant idea to return triumphantly at their own funeral. His successful persuasion of the boys proves, once again, his understanding of psychology. Tom knows that Huck and Joe too are curious about how they will be missed.

Unlike Tom, who cares very much about appearances, Huck does not concern himself with what others think of him. His existence outside of society permits him to deny its expectations, and he does not feel the need to show off or fit in like the rest of the St. Petersburg boys. In fact, Huck seems genuinely uncomfortable as the recipient of affection. When, amid the joy following the boys' return, Aunt Polly welcomes Huck with a hug, the self-sufficient Huck is genuinely embarrassed.

Chapters 18–20

Summary—Chapter 18: Tom Reveals His Dream Secret

The morning after Tom returns from the island, Aunt Polly rebukes him for having made her suffer so much and for not having given her some hint that he was not actually dead. Tom argues that doing so would have spoiled the whole adventure, but he admits that he "dreamed" about everyone back in town. Telling her his dream, Tom relates everything he saw and overheard when he crossed the river and sneaked into the house a few nights earlier. Aunt Polly seems amazed by the power of Tom's vision and forgives him for not having visited her. Sid, meanwhile, wonders suspiciously how this dream could be so precise and detailed.

At school, Tom is declared a hero and basks in the adulation of his peers. He decides to ignore Becky and instead pays attention to Amy Lawrence again. When Becky realizes that he is ignoring her, she gets within earshot and begins issuing invitations to a picnic. Soon she has asked the whole class to come except Tom and Amy. They go off together, leaving Becky to stew in jealousy.

At recess, however, Becky manages to turn the tables by agreeing to look at a picture book with Alfred Temple, the new boy from the city with whom Tom fights at the beginning of the novel. Tom grows jealous and becomes bored with Amy. With a great sense of relief, he heads home alone for lunch. Once Tom is gone, Becky drops Alfred, who, when he realizes what has transpired, pours ink on Tom's spelling book to get him in trouble. Becky sees Alfred commit the act and considers warning Tom in the hopes of mending their troubles. But, overcome by Tom's recent cruelness to her, she decides instead that Tom deserves a whipping and that she will hate him forever.

Summary—Chapter 19: The Cruelty of "I Didn't Think"

Back home, Aunt Polly has learned from Mrs. Harper that Tom's dream was a fake and that he came home one night and spied on them. Aunt Polly scolds him for making her look like a fool in front of Mrs. Harper and then asks why he came home but still did nothing to relieve everyone's sorrow. Tom replies that he was going to leave a message for her, but he was afraid it would spoil the surprise, so he left it in his pocket. She sends him back to school and goes to look in the jacket that he wore to Jackson's Island, resolving not to be angry if the message is not there. When she finds it, she breaks down in tears and says, "I could forgive the boy, now, if he'd committed a million sins!"

SUMMARY—CHAPTER 20: TOM TAKES BECKY'S PUNISHMENT

Back at school, Tom attempts a reconciliation with Becky, but she blows him off and looks forward to seeing him whipped for the inky spelling book. She proceeds to find a key in the lock of the teacher's desk drawer; the drawer contains a book that only the teacher, Mr. Dobbins, is allowed to read. She opens it and discovers that it is an anatomy textbook that Mr. Dobbins possesses since his true ambition is to be a doctor. She opens it to the front page, which shows a naked figure, and at that moment Tom enters. His entry startles her so much that she rips the page. She begins to cry, blames him for making her rip it, and realizes now that *she* will be whipped.

The class files in, and Tom stands stoically for his own whipping, assuming that he must have spilled the ink himself accidentally. Mr. Dobbins finds the ripped book and begins to grill each member of the class in turn. When he reaches Becky, she seems ready to break down, but she is saved when Tom rises and declares, "I done it!"—thus incurring a second whipping but becoming a hero again in Becky's eyes.

ANALYSIS—CHAPTERS 18–20

In these chapters, Tom fluctuates between petty, immature behavior—lying to his aunt about his alleged dream and trying to make Becky jealous at the expense of Amy's feelings—and nobler conduct—saving Becky from punishment. The fact that Tom's story about his dream fools his aunt but not Sid may ironically indicate that in some way children are more perceptive than adults. On the other hand, perhaps Aunt Polly is deceived because true maturity includes love and the forgiveness that comes along with it. Perhaps Sid is too morally immature to understand that such trickery is excusable in a person that one loves.

Once Tom realizes the damage he has done, he feels remorse for the second time in the novel, which indicates that his moral growth is continuing. He feels genuine affection for Aunt Polly and wants to secure her approval. His manipulation of her seems to happen almost instinctively, as he gets carried away by his own flights of fancy.

The snubbing war between Tom and Becky forms a counterpart to the make-believe military battle fought between generals Tom and Joe early in the novel. Descriptions of the elaborate strategies

Tom and Becky employ to make each other jealous make up the bulk of these chapters. Both behave in a petty, childish fashion, trying to prove to one another how little each needs the other. Until Tom takes Becky's punishment, the two remain trapped in this cycle of nasty behavior. Tom's act of self-sacrifice breaks the cycle and enables the pair to reunite. By taking Becky's whipping and winning her back, Tom also brings his pirate adventure to its full conclusion, since it begins with Becky's rejection of him.

Twain directs our sympathy in these chapters toward Amy and Alfred, whom Tom and Becky use and then discard. Both characters, who vanish from the novel after Chapter 18, remain tools. Not only are they tools for Tom and Becky in their love war, but they are also rather dull characters for Twain himself—he doesn't even consider going beyond the letter "A" in giving them names. Mr. Dobbins too serves as nothing more than a tool for Tom's development. Mr. Dobbins's threatening authority, although undermined in our eyes by the discovery of his secret desire to be a doctor and his humorous obsession with his medical textbook, allows Tom a chance to act heroically.

CHAPTERS 21–24

SUMMARY—CHAPTER 21: ELOQUENCE—AND THE MASTER'S GILDED DOME

Summer has almost arrived and the schoolchildren are restless. Mr. Dobbins becomes even more harsh in his discipline, provoking the boys to conspire against him. At the end of the year, the town gathers in the schoolhouse for the "Examination," in which students recite speeches and poems and engage in spelling and geography competitions. Tom struggles through "Give me liberty or give me death," finally succumbing to stage fright, and a series of young ladies then recites the hilariously awful poems and essays they have written. Finally, the schoolmaster turns to the blackboard to draw a map of the United States for the geography class, and at that moment a blindfolded cat is lowered from the rafters by a string. The animal claws at the air and yanks off Mr. Dobbins's wig, revealing a bald head that the sign-painter's boy gilded while Mr. Dobbins slept off a bout of drinking.

SUMMARY—CHAPTER 22: HUCK FINN QUOTES SCRIPTURE

At the beginning of summer, Tom joins the Cadets of Temperance in order to wear one of their showy uniforms. Unfortunately, to join he must swear off smoking, tobacco chewing, and cursing—prohibitions that prove very difficult. He resolves to hang on until Judge Frazier, the justice of the peace, dies, because then he can wear his red sash in the public funeral. When the judge recovers, Tom resigns from the Cadets. The judge suffers a relapse and dies that night.

Vacation begins to drag. Becky Thatcher has gone to the town of Constantinople to stay with her parents, and the various circuses, parades, and minstrel shows that pass through town provide only temporary entertainment. The secret of Dr. Robinson's murder still tugs at Tom's conscience. Tom then gets the measles, and when he begins to recover, he discovers that a revival has swept through the town, leaving all his friends suddenly religious. That night brings a terrible thunderstorm, which Tom assumes must be directed at him as punishment for his sinful ways. The next day he has a relapse of the measles and stays in bed for three weeks. When he is finally on his feet again, Tom finds that all his friends have reverted to their former, impious ways.

Summary—Chapter 23: The Salvation of Muff Potter

Muff Potter's trial approaches, and Tom and Huck agonize about whether they should reveal what they know. They agree that Injun Joe would kill them, so they continue to help Potter in small ways, bringing him tobacco and matches and feeling guilty when he thanks them for their friendship. The trial finally arrives, and Injun Joe gives his account of the events. A series of witnesses testifies to Potter's peculiar behavior, and in each case Potter's lawyer declines to cross-examine. Finally, Potter's lawyer calls Tom Sawyer as a witness for the defense, much to everyone's amazement. Tom, deeply frightened, takes the witness stand and tells the court what he saw that night. When he reaches the point in the story where Injun Joe stabs the doctor, Injun Joe leaps from his seat, pulls free of everyone, and escapes through a window.

Summary—Chapter 24: Splendid Days and Fearsome Nights

> *Tom was a glittering hero once more—the pet of the old, the envy of the young. . . . There were some that believed he would be President, yet, if he escaped hanging.*
> (See QUOTATIONS, p. 56)

Tom is acclaimed as a hero and enjoys the adulation and gratitude of Muff Potter and the rest of the town during the day. At night, however, he is tormented by visions of Injun Joe coming to kill him. Injun Joe has vanished, despite the town's and a detective's best efforts to locate and capture him.

ANALYSIS — CHAPTERS 21–24

Mr. Dobbins's humiliation at the hands of the sign-painter's boy and the revelation that he drinks too much links him with the Sunday school superintendent and the minister as a person in a position of power who falls victim to Twain's deft satire. Dobbins is a prime example of an authority figure who, ironically, has no true authority, because he is clearly dissatisfied with who he is. Both Mr. Dobbins's obsession with his anatomy textbook and his false hair manifest his desire to be something that he is not.

In a footnote, Twain claims that the flowery, overstated compositions presented in the Examination scene are not his own creations but rather "are taken without alteration from a volume entitled 'Prose and Poetry, by a Western Lady.'" One composition begins "Dark and tempestuous was night" in a pretentious version of the clichéd first line, "It was a dark and stormy night." Twain is criticizing the shallowness of small-town intellectual pretension, but his footnote suggests that his criticism is specifically directed toward women, and this scene is somewhat misogynistic (woman-hating). However one may interpret it, the Examination scene criticizes the same flaw to which the character of Dobbins falls prey: trying to be something one is not.

Like the Sunday school scene in which Tom claims a Bible, Twain ends the Examination chapter with a shocking event—the cat lifting the wig—but avoids describing the event's aftermath. There may be several reasons for Twain's omission of the specifics, but one explanation concerns the novel's universality. Twain's criticism is generally directed toward universal human foibles; importantly, he leave blanks for us to fill in, so that each reader ponders the events within his or her own frame of reference.

In Chapter 22, Twain again pokes fun at the fickleness of the townspeople's religious belief. When a revival sweeps town, all the boys "get religion," but they go back to their old ways within a few weeks. Tom's understanding of God evolves out of his superstitious way of viewing the world—when a thunderstorm strikes, he believes that God has aimed it at him as a personal punishment.

Tom's decision to testify at Muff Potter's trial marks an important moment in his process of maturation from childhood to adulthood.

SUMMARY & ANALYSIS

His fear for his physical safety and his superstitious unwillingness to go back on his blood oath with Joe Harper are what have kept him from doing the right thing. Both are sentiments associated with childhood. While Twain does not give us a direct depiction of Tom's internal moral crisis, he builds an atmosphere of increasing anxiety and indicates that Tom's silence may have serious implications for the wrongly accused Muff Potter. When Tom eventually changes his priorities and acts out of concern for Muff instead of out of concern for himself, he conquers his fear and achieves a greater level of maturity.

If *Tom Sawyer* were a simple bildungsroman, a narrative of moral and psychological growth, then Tom's decision to testify would be an appropriate ending. However, *Tom Sawyer* is also an adventure story, and to add suspense and danger to the plot, Twain allows Injun Joe to escape. Psychologically, Tom may be on the road to adulthood, but he still has to conquer Injun Joe outside the courtroom before his adventures can conclude.

CHAPTERS 25–26

SUMMARY — CHAPTER 25: SEEKING THE BURIED TREASURE

One day Tom has a desire to hunt for buried treasure. He encounters Huck Finn, and the two discuss possible places to find treasure, what form the loot might take, and how kings have hundreds of diamonds but only one name. They then set off for the nearest dead-limbed tree, since such trees are typical hiding places for treasure. When they arrive, they discuss what they would do with the treasure. Huck plans to spend it all on pie and soda, and Tom decides that he would get married, an idea that Huck finds absurd.

That afternoon, the boys dig in a number of places around the tree but find nothing. At first, Tom blames a witch, and he then realizes that they are going about it all wrong: they need to find where the shadow of the tree limb falls at midnight. They return that night and dig for a time, again without result. Eventually frustration and fear of the darkened woods make them give up, but they hesitantly agree to try next in the "ha'nted" house, a deserted building nearby.

SUMMARY — CHAPTER 26: REAL ROBBERS SEIZE
THE BOX OF GOLD

The following day, Tom and Huck set out for the house, only to realize that it is Friday—the most unlucky day of the week. They decide to pretend they are Robin Hood for the rest of the afternoon and make their way to the haunted house on Saturday. They explore the house's deserted ground floor, then head upstairs as two mysterious men enter downstairs. One is "a ragged, unkempt creature, with nothing very pleasant about his face"; the other is a deaf and mute Spaniard with a long white beard and green goggles who has been hanging around St. Petersburg recently. The boys watch the two strangers through the floorboards. When the deaf and mute Spaniard speaks, the boys recognize his voice—it is Injun Joe's.

Terrified, the boys listen as the two men talk about criminal activities, including a "dangerous" job that Injun Joe plans. After a while, the two men doze off. Tom wants to leave, but Huck is too frightened that the men might wake up. Eventually, the men wake and prepare to go. Before they leave, they bury some money they have stolen—$600 in silver—because it is too heavy to carry. While hiding it, they encounter an iron box, which they unearth using the tools that the boys left on the ground floor. The box is full of gold coins, and the boys think, ecstatically, that the two men will rebury it. However, Injun Joe notices that the boys' tools are new and have fresh earth on them, and he decides that someone must be hanging around the house. Injun Joe even starts to go upstairs, but the steps collapse under his weight. He gives up, deciding to take the treasure to another hiding place: "Number Two—under the cross."

The men leave with the loot, and Huck and Tom descend, wishing furiously that they had not left their tools behind for Injun Joe to find. They resolve to keep an eye out for the "Spaniard" in the hopes of following him to "Number Two." Then the awful thought occurs to Tom that perhaps Injun Joe's planned "job" will be on Tom and Huck. The boys talk it over, and Huck decides that since only Tom testified, Injun Joe's wrath will probably be directed only at him. Huck's words, of course, offer little comfort to Tom.

ANALYSIS—CHAPTERS 25–26
Initially, Tom's desire to hunt for treasure appears to be just another juvenile adventure along the lines of the boys' trip to Jackson's Island. It is only when Injun Joe appears that we realize that the narrative is no longer skipping from adventure to adventure but is instead driving toward an ending. By offering different settings in which the action unfolds, Twain allows us to see Tom's developing maturity and the effects that it has on his interactions with his friends, Becky, and his family. Twain allows us to trace this development in these

various relationships without prioritizing one over the others, thus establishing the importance of each facet in a boy's life.

Tom has pretty much abandoned Joe by this point in the novel. When he wants to play Robin Hood earlier in the novel, he goes out with Joe; now, however, the stronger, more well-defined character of Huck has taken Joe's place. Whereas Joe and Tom seem to be roughly equivalent characters, Huck is clearly more independent (given his way of life, he has to be) and in certain ways more mature than Tom. Despite his relative maturity, Huck nevertheless defers to Tom's imagination and initiative when it comes to planning their activities. He does so largely because he is slightly in awe of Tom's book-learning and his superior knowledge about the rules governing their various activities, even when he does not fully understand what they mean.

Although Huck generally seems tougher than Tom, when the robbers are asleep, Huck is the one who is too afraid to move. This sudden fear may seem out of character, but, in general, Huck's survival seems the result of his *flight* from difficulties, so it makes sense that he would attempt to avoid conflict and danger. Tom, on the other hand, tends to confront his problems and attempts to devise clever solutions. In a way, Huck is more of a realist—more likely than Tom to recognize the point at which an imaginative game ends and real life, with its real dangers, begins.

Twain raises the level of suspense by suggesting that Injun Joe may be seeking revenge on Tom and Huck. It is important to note that Injun Joe's unnamed partner is more of a device for Twain than a true sidekick. It takes a certain level of maturity to develop a true partnership. Tom develops this maturity as the novel progresses, but Injun Joe certainly does not. Injun Joe's partner serves merely as a device to enable dialogue, which gives the boys—and us—access to Injun Joe's thoughts. Were Injun Joe alone in the house, there would be no conversation for the boys to overhear. The disclosures Injun Joe makes and the gaps he leaves generate the mystery of this portion of the narrative.

Once the hidden gold is introduced into the plot, the novel becomes more an adventure story and less a realistic portrayal of boyhood. Twain may also have chosen to introduce the hidden gold to provide a grown-up counterpart to the trinket-for-ticket exchanges that take place in the early chapters. Here, Tom's newfound maturity has as a counterpart a larger, more intricate economic system—one in which there is considerably more at stake.

CHAPTERS 27–29

SUMMARY—CHAPTER 27: TREMBLING ON THE TRAIL

The next morning, after a night of troubled sleep, Tom considers the possibility that events of the previous day were a dream. He finds Huck, and Huck rids him of this idea. The two boys speculate about where hiding place "Number Two" might be, deciding that "Two" probably refers to a room number in one of the town's two taverns. Tom visits the first tavern and learns that a lawyer occupies room number two. In the second tavern, room number two remains locked all the time. The tavern-keeper's son claims that no one ever enters or leaves the room except at night. He claims to have noticed a light on in the room the previous night. The boys decide to find all the keys they can and try them in the room's back door. Meanwhile, if Injun Joe appears, the boys plan to tail him to see where he goes, in case they are wrong about the room.

SUMMARY—CHAPTER 28: IN THE LAIR OF INJUN JOE

On Thursday, the boys make their way to the tavern. Tom slips inside, and Huck waits for him. Suddenly Tom rushes by, shouting for them to run. Neither stops until he reaches the other end of the village, where Tom recounts that he found the door unlocked and Injun Joe asleep on the floor, surrounded by whiskey bottles. The tavern is a "Temperance Tavern," meaning that it purportedly serves no alcohol. The boys realize that the room must be off-limits because it is where the tavern secretly serves whiskey. The boys decide that Huck will watch the room every night. If Injun Joe leaves, Huck will get Tom, who will sneak in and take the treasure.

SUMMARY—CHAPTER 29: HUCK SAVES THE WIDOW

The next day, the Thatchers return from Constantinople. When Tom sees Becky, he learns that her picnic is planned for the following day, so the Injun Joe predicament drops to secondary importance. The children plan to go downriver to a famous cavern, and Becky's mother tells Becky to spend the night with one of her friends who lives near the ferry. Tom then persuades Becky to disobey her mother and go with him to the Widow Douglas's house instead, where the kind woman will probably give them ice cream and let them spend the night.

As they take the ferry down the river, Tom worries briefly that Injun Joe may go out that night, and he may miss the action. But the promise of fun with Becky soon drives such worries from his mind.

The children arrive at a "woody hollow," play in the forest, and eat lunch. Afterward, they climb up to McDougal's cave and spend the afternoon excitedly exploring the passages. They stagger out that evening happily covered in clay and board the ferry for home.

Huck sees the ferry arrive in town, and a short time later he sees two men pass him carrying a box. Assuming them to be Injun Joe and his companion, he decides that there is no time to fetch Tom—the two men are escaping with the gold. He follows them to the Widow Douglas's house, where Injun Joe describes to his friend how he plans to slit the widow's nostrils and notch her ears like a sow as revenge for an incident in which her husband, then justice of the peace, had him horsewhipped for vagrancy.

While the two villains wait for the widow's light to go out, Huck races down the hill to the house of an old Welshman and his sons. They let him in, and when he tells them what is about to happen, they seize their guns and rush toward the widow's house. Huck follows them for a time, hears a burst of gunfire, and then flees for his life.

SUMMARY & ANALYSIS

ANALYSIS — CHAPTERS 27–29

Chapter 27, which opens with Tom's belief that his adventures were only a dream, prepares us for the dreamlike quality of the novel's conclusion. Before Tom and Huck find out about Injun Joe's treasure, St. Petersburg seems a safe, sleepy town with year-round summery weather perfect for children's make-believe and games. However, once fantasy adventures of piracy and Robin Hood turn into real encounters with outlaws, murder, and stolen treasure, Tom and Huck seem well prepared to handle the scenario precisely because of their many rehearsals. Although much of the novel concerns Tom's gradual acclimation to the adult world, the surprising plot twist brought about by Tom and Huck's discovery of Injun Joe's plan seems to reaffirm their childhood activities and to suggest that these imaginative activities should not be abandoned as soon as adult responsibilities emerge.

Twain has already poked fun at church, school, and Sunday school, so his unveiling of the Temperance movement's hypocrisy—the "Temperance Tavern" serves alcohol in a secret room—follows naturally. Because the novel focuses on Tom's journey toward adulthood, and because Twain views the adult world as hypocritical and pretentious, it can be argued that Twain views Tom's maturation as an unfortunate loss of freedom and honesty. However, Twain seems to be redefining the concept of maturity. Whereas conventional understanding links maturity with adulthood, Twain distinguishes between real maturity—the kind Tom displays when he testifies against Injun Joe and saves Becky from punishment—and the false maturity of the Temperance Tavern and the Sunday school. The older townspeople may be more learned than Tom by virtue of their age, and thus more intellectually mature, but Twain makes no similar correlation between age and moral maturity.

When Tom leaves Huck by himself to handle Injun Joe because he is excited by the prospect of picnicking with Becky, he behaves immaturely and gets himself into trouble. In Chapter 30, we find out that Tom and Becky haven't actually gone to the Widow Douglas's house; they are lost in the cave. The stage seems set for a final confrontation between Tom and Injun Joe at the Widow Douglas's, but Huck, not Tom, is to prove the hero. Tom has been the planner all along, persuading the reluctant Huck to go along with his schemes. By staying when Tom irresponsibly leaves for the picnic, Huck finally assumes control of the Injun Joe plot and proves his superior maturity.

Chapters 30–32

Summary—Chapter 30: Tom and Becky in the Cave

The next morning, a Sunday, Huck creeps to the Welshman's house and learns that the whole town is out looking for the deaf and mute Spaniard and his companion—both of whom the old man and his sons chased away the night before. (The Welshman does not yet know the Spaniard's true identity.) Huck then describes how he followed the intruders the previous night. He tries not to mention the treasure, but eventually he describes the deaf and mute man's speech and so has to admit that the Spaniard is actually Injun Joe. The Welshman tells him that the package the two men were carrying contained burglary tools, which relieves Huck considerably, because it means that the treasure must still be in the tavern.

Soon everyone has heard about the events at the widow's house, but the Welshman keeps the identity of the boy who saved the widow a secret, in order to make it a great surprise. At church that morning, everyone discusses the excitement, and then Mrs. Thatcher asks Mrs. Harper where Becky is. Mrs. Harper says that Becky did not stay with her, and then Aunt Polly appears, wondering where Tom is. Eventually everyone realizes, to a collective horror, that Tom and Becky must still be in the cave.

A search party is organized and sets out for the cave immediately. The day drags on with no word from the missing children, and Huck, meanwhile, acquires a fever. The Widow Douglas, who remains ignorant of Huck's actions the previous night, takes care of him. Eventually, the searchers in the cave begin to give up—the only traces found of the children are the words "BECKY & TOM," written on the cave walls in candle-smoke soot, and one of Becky's ribbons.

In the days that follow, the town discovers that Temperance Tavern serves liquor. When Huck wakes from his feverish sleep at one point, he asks Widow Douglas if anything has been found at the Temperance Tavern. She tells him that alcohol has been discovered and the tavern shut down, so Huck assumes the treasure is gone. Tom and Becky remain lost.

Summary—Chapter 31: Found and Lost Again

The story returns to Tom and Becky on the day of the picnic. They wander away from the larger group, exploring and using smoke to make marks on the walls so that they can find their way back. Eventually, they come to a large room filled with bats, and the bats attack them and chase them into unknown passages. After escaping the bats, they realize how far from the others they are and decide to go back, but they cannot go the way they came, as the bats are blocking it. Tom chooses another passage to follow, and, after a while, they realize they are completely lost. Tom hasn't made any marks, and even finding the bats again seems impossible.

The couple wanders on, occasionally calling for help. Becky sleeps for a time. When she wakes up, they realize that their parents will not miss them until the following day. Despair sets in for a while. They then hear the voices of rescuers and call in reply. The search parties do not hear them, and the children find their way blocked by crevices and pitfalls. The voices grow fainter and eventually cease. The children grope their way to a spring and sit down, knowing they will soon run out of candles.

While Becky sleeps, Tom explores side passages with the aid of a kite line. He sees a candle on the other side of a pitfall and then sees Injun Joe holding it and retreats in terror. Not wanting to frighten Becky, he doesn't tell her what he has seen, and he continues to explore other passages.

Summary—Chapter 32: "Turn Out! They're Found!"

Tuesday night arrives, and Tom and Becky still have not been found. Only Judge Thatcher and a few companions continue searching the cave. Then, in the middle of the night, news arrives that the children have turned up, and St. Petersburg celebrates. The children are taken to the Thatcher house, where a weakened Tom describes their escape. The kite string ran out while he was exploring a gallery, and he was about to turn back when he saw a speck of daylight in the distance. He abandoned the string and crawled forward until he could push through a hole and see the Mississippi River. He then went back and found Becky, and from there, the two crawled out and went to the nearest house, five miles downstream from the cave.

Judge Thatcher and the last searchers learn that the children have been found. Tom and Becky are bedridden for most of the rest of the week. Tom goes to see the invalid Huck that Friday, but the Widow Douglas warns him to avoid any upsetting topics. Tom learns about Injun Joe's attempt against the widow and also hears that Injun Joe's companion was found drowned while trying to escape.

Two weeks after he finds his way out of the cave, Tom talks to Judge Thatcher and is told that the door of the cave has been shut and bolted from the outside to prevent anyone else from getting lost. Tom becomes horrified and tells the judge that Injun Joe remains in the caverns.

ANALYSIS — CHAPTERS 30–32

At the end of Chapter 29, the novel seems to be moving toward a final confrontation at the Widow Douglas's house, but that resolution is thwarted when the Welshman chases off Injun Joe. Twain also removes Huck from the action by having him get sick. This temporary elimination of two main characters leaves the novel's focus on Tom and Becky, lost in the cave. Twain narrates the episode of their entrapment with superb realism and suspense. We experience vividly their hunger and their fear, their swings between hope and despair.

We can view the cave scene as a miniature version of Tom's entire journey toward maturity. Tom's immaturity and his lack of foresight lead him and Becky to stay away from the others for too long and to forget to make marks on the walls so that they can find their way back to the entrance. Once they are lost, however, Tom rises to the occasion. He assumes responsibility for his mistakes, behaves generously toward Becky, and takes practical measures like saving candles and finding a spring to sit by once the candles are nearly gone. Tom takes the initiative to explore the side passages around the spring, while Becky, who is less rugged, sleeps or lies in a daze.

Eventually, Tom's persistence and continued resourcefulness lead him and Becky out of the cave. As Tom matures, his adaptability develops, along with his willingness to accept his own mistakes.

Tom's dramatic nature and active imagination have made him terribly afraid of Injun Joe, but we have every reason to believe that Injun Joe may be more afraid than Tom. Tom's explanation for Injun Joe's flight from him in the cave is that Injun Joe didn't recognize him. Tom is convinced that Injun Joe wants to kill him for having testified at his trial, but it is likely that Injun Joe really doesn't care too much about Tom. Rather, Injun Joe seems more concerned about his own fate.

Although Twain relates Tom and Becky's three days in the cave from the points of view of Tom and Becky, he depicts their climactic escape from the cave from the point of view of the townspeople, who have been suffering while searching for three days. When Tom and Becky return, the town explodes in celebration, in a manner that parallels the boys' return from Jackson's Island earlier in the novel. In both cases, the town believes Tom to be dead, and in both cases, we see the children's reappearance through the eyes of the community—the angle from which the suspense is greatest.

CHAPTERS 33–CONCLUSION

SUMMARY—CHAPTER 33: THE FATE OF INJUN JOE

A party rushes down to the cave, unlocks the door, and finds Injun Joe starved to death inside. He evidently has eaten the few bats he could catch, used every candle stump he could find, and made a cup out of rock and placed it under a dripping stalactite to catch a spoonful of water a day. "Injun Joe's Cup," Twain informs us, has since become one of the chief tourist attractions in the cave.

The morning after Injun Joe's funeral, Tom tells Huck his theory that the gold never was in Room No. 2 at the Temperance Tavern. Instead, he believes that it remains hidden in the cave. That afternoon, the boys take a raft down to the place where Tom and Becky exited the cave and crawl inside. Tom comments on how much he wants to start a gang of robbers and use this part of the cave as a hideout. The boys discuss how grand it would be to be robbers and eventually reach the place where Tom encountered Injun Joe.

Tom points out a cross that is burned on the wall of the cave and tells Huck that this, not the tavern, must be where the gold is hidden. Huck becomes frightened that Injun Joe's ghost could be lurking around, but Tom points out that the cross would keep him away. Comforted by Tom's words, Huck helps him search the area. The boys find nothing and decide to dig under the rock. There they find a collection of guns, moccasins, a belt, and the treasure.

The boys decide to leave the guns behind, reasoning that they will be useful for their band of robbers in the future. They drag the gold out of the cavern and put it on their raft back to St. Petersburg. On their way to hide the treasure, however, they encounter the Welshman, who insists that they accompany him to a party at the Widow Douglas's house. He sees the box they are lugging but assumes they have been collecting old iron.

SUMMARY — CHAPTER 34: FLOODS OF GOLD

Nearly every person of importance in the village has gathered at the Widow Douglas's house. While the boys change into nice clothes, Huck tells Tom that he wants to escape out the window because he cannot stand such a large crowd. Tom tells him not to worry. Sid comes in and informs them that the party is being given in honor of the Welshman, Mr. Jones, and his sons, and that Mr. Jones plans to surprise everyone by announcing that Huck was the real hero. Sid then says, in a self-satisfied way, that the surprise will fall flat because he has already spoiled it. Tom yells at Sid for being such a nasty sneak and chases him out of the room.

At the supper table, Mr. Jones tells his secret and everyone pretends to be surprised. Widow Douglas then announces that she plans to give Huck a home and educate him. Tom bursts out, "Huck don't need it. Huck's rich." Everyone chuckles at the joke, and Tom runs outside and brings in the gold. Everyone is shocked. When the money is counted, it adds up to over twelve thousand dollars.

SUMMARY — CHAPTER 35: RESPECTABLE HUCK JOINS THE GANG

> *Huck Finn's wealth and the fact that he was now under the Widow Douglas's protection introduced him into society — no, dragged him into it, hurled him into it — and his sufferings were almost more than he could bear.*
> *(See QUOTATIONS, p. 57)*

The news of the gold shocks the village and inspires dozens of treasure hunters. The money is invested and provides both boys an allowance of almost a dollar a day—equal to the minister's salary.

Becky tells her father about how noble Tom has been, and the judge decides that Tom should go to the National Military Academy and then become a lawyer. Huck, meanwhile, suffers terribly under the burden of being civilized. He bears wearing clean clothes, sleeping in sheets, and eating with a knife and fork for three weeks; he then runs away. The town searches for him, but to no avail. Tom finds him, eventually, sleeping in an abandoned slaughterhouse, and Huck tells his friend that he simply is not cut out for a respectable life. The Widow Douglas makes him dress nicely and forbids him to spit, swear, or smoke.

Tom replies that Huck can do as he pleases, but if he wants to join Tom's gang of robbers, he has to be respectable. Otherwise, he says, Huck's sour reputation will drag down the whole gang. Huck agrees to try the widow's house again for a month—provided that Tom allows him to belong to the gang.

Summary — Conclusion

Twain writes that the story must end here because it is strictly a story about a boy. Were the story to continue, he states, it would quickly become the story of a man. He adds that most of the characters in the story are still alive and that he might one day explore how they turned out.

Analysis — Chapters 33–Conclusion

In a way, the town rewards Tom for his disobedience. It hails him as a hero in relation to three actions that are marked by mischief—his return from Jackson's Island, his testimony against Injun Joe, and his return from the caverns. A model boy would never get lost in a cave or be able to lie "upon a sofa with an eager auditory about him and [tell] the history of the wonderful adventure." Tom's adventuresome spirit leads him into risks that others would not attempt, and his payoff is heroism.

Twain's message, however, is not that disobedience is a virtue. Others who disobey, such as Injun Joe, fall prey to Twain's criticism without any heroic tempering. Although Injun Joe, Tom, and Huck are all inherently mischievous, Injun Joe harms others to satisfy his inclinations. Tom and Huck, though true to their mischievous natures, never allow themselves to harm others—they feel bad even about stealing bacon. A third category of characters in the novel includes those who obey outwardly but harbor malevolence on the inside—Sid, for example. These hypocrites are the subtle antiheroes of the novel.

After his triumphant return from the cave, Tom regains his sense of perspective and leads Huck back to the cave to find the treasure. Their plan for a "robber band," which Tom will in fact establish in *The Adventures of Huckleberry Finn,* marks a return to the world of boyhood fantasy, as it resembles the pirate band they create on Jackson's Island and the outlaws they pretend to be in Sherwood Forest. Tom and Huck also return to their boyhood mind-set in the cave when they argue about superstition. But the way Tom deflects Huck's arguments, enabling the conversation topic to move beyond superstition so that the boys can get the gold, displays his increasing maturity.

When the Widow Douglas adopts Huck, not only his treasure but also his life become subject to adult control. As Huck and Tom change upstairs in the Widow Douglas's house before her dinner party, Huck is so worried about the life that awaits him that he attempts to persuade Tom to escape. Tom dismisses Huck's fears, promising to "take care of [Huck]," but Huck's worries prove well founded. Not long after he and Tom go downstairs together, the secret of their riches is revealed, and they are quickly ushered into the daunting adult world.

Tom is far more ready than Huck to enter the adult community. When we first meet Huck, Twain writes, "Tom envied him his gaudy outcast condition"; now Tom urges Huck to embrace respectability. The Tom we meet in the first chapter, with jam on his face and mischief on his mind, has given way to a boy who defends the adult order by preventing Huck from escaping out the window. Tom is not yet a man and still has plans for a robber gang, but Judge Thatcher is already talking about sending him to the military academy and law school. When Tom finds Huck after he has attempted to run away from the Widow Douglas's house, he couches his appeal to return in the language of childhood, telling Huck that he needs to be respectable to be in the robber band. But we sense that Tom is using this rhetoric to appeal to Huck because, with his newfound money and status, Tom has a stake in adult society that he wants to defend.

Twain's closing words wrap up matters for Tom and Huck and usher them into adult society without actually showing them as adults. Their gold, which has been pursued without the adults' knowledge as a kind of game, is no longer a game. The gold has become a business so serious that Judge Thatcher, the most significant and authoritative figure in the adult hierarchy, assumes control of it.

Gone are Huck's plans to spend it *all* on candy, although on a dollar a day, he will happily be able to enjoy his share of sweets.

There is a note of sadness in Twain's concluding statement that Tom's story will soon become "the history of a *man*." The woods and fields around St. Petersburg, where Tom plays Robin Hood, pirates, and Indians, have given way to the world of money invested at interest. The freedom of childhood, represented by Huck, has been absorbed by the adult order. The novel, which mixes a nostalgia for the carefree days of youth with illuminating criticism of adult society, cannot but regret the conclusion of childhood, even while recognizing—as Tom tries to enable Huck to recognize—the importance of moving toward maturity and sophistication.

Important Quotations Explained

1.   I ain't doing my duty by that boy, and that's the Lord's truth, goodness knows. Spare the rod and spile the child, as the Good Book says. I'm a-laying up sin and suffering for us both, I know. He's full of the Old Scratch, but laws-a-me! he's my own dead sister's boy, poor thing, and I ain't got the heart to lash him, somehow. Every time I let him off, my conscience does hurt me so, and every time I hit him my old heart most breaks.

This quotation is from Chapter 1, when Tom has just escaped Aunt Polly's grasp once again. Aunt Polly's mixture of amusement and frustration at Tom's antics is characteristic of her good humor. She attempts to discipline Tom out of a sense of duty more than out of any real indignation. In fact, she often seems to admire Tom's cleverness and his vivacity. Her inner conflict about her treatment of Tom is summed up in the final sentence of this passage.

   The faithful re-creation of regional dialects is a characteristic element of Twain's style. Aunt Polly uses a colloquial vocabulary and pronunciation that may be difficult for a reader unfamiliar with these speech patterns. Twain's minute attention to language is an important aspect of his realism—his project of capturing the uniqueness of American frontier life. Twain carefully studied the speech of his local Missouri community and experimented with different ways of rendering it in writing. Furthermore, he attended closely to the internal variations in speech even within such a small town as Hannibal (rendered in his fiction as St. Petersburg). The differences between the language of rich people and poor people, and between the language of blacks and whites, often find expression in Twain's dialogue. In addition to its distinctive idiom and accent, Aunt Polly's speech is peppered with clichés and folk wisdom, mixing Scripture and local sayings in a way that gives structure and meaning to her experience.

2.   "Oh come, now, you don't mean to let on that you like it?"
     The brush continued to move.
     "Like it? Well I don't see why I oughtn't to like it. Does a boy get a chance to whitewash a fence every day?"
     That put the thing in a new light. Ben stopped nibbling his apple. Tom swept his brush daintily back and forth—stepped back to note the effect—added a touch here and there—criticized the effect again—Ben watching every move and getting more and more interested, more and more absorbed. Presently he said:
     "Say, Tom, let me whitewash a little."

This interchange between Ben Rogers and Tom occurs during the whitewashing episode from Chapter 2. One of Tom's earliest exploits in the novel, the whitewashing scam gives us a thorough initial look at Tom's ingenious character. Most evident in this dialogue with Ben Rogers is Tom's consummate skill as an actor and his instinctive understanding of human behavior. In these moments of prankish virtuosity, Tom always keeps one step ahead of his victims, anticipating their reactions and cornering them verbally into the response he desires. In painting these scenes, Twain draws on the American folk tradition of the trickster. (The Br'er Rabbit tales are another well-known example of this type of story.)

This episode also gives Twain a chance to advance the idea that certain values are as much a matter of convention as anything. The moral with which Twain concludes this amusing scene is, "Work consists of whatever a body is *obliged* to do, and . . . [p]lay consists of whatever a body is not obliged to do." The arbitrariness of many conventions and the absurdity with which people desire things just because they are forbidden are facts of life that Twain scrutinizes again and again in the novel.

QUOTATIONS

3.   Mr. Walters fell to "showing off," with all sorts of official bustlings and activities. . . . The librarian "showed off"—running hither and thither with his arms full of books. . . . The young lady teachers "showed off". . . . The young gentlemen teachers "showed off". . . . The little girls "showed off" in various ways, and the little boys "showed off" with such diligence that the air was thick with paper wads and the murmur of scufflings. And above it all the great man sat and beamed a majestic judicial smile upon all the house, and warmed himself in the sun of his own grandeur—for he was "showing off," too.

This Sunday school scene from Chapter 4 shows the height of Twain's leveling satire. While Twain makes explicit jabs at the religious spirit and the structures of organized religion elsewhere in the novel, in this scene he directs his mockery toward human nature in a more generalized way. Much of the comic effect of this scene stems from the uniformity of the ridiculous behavior exhibited by teachers, students, boys, and girls. So strong is the human need to impress and to win approval that not even Judge Thatcher is exempt from the temptation to "show off." Twain suggests that the desire to stand out is universal, which means that in their efforts to distinguish themselves, people wind up all looking alike.

    For the adults, "showing off" means attempting to conceal the rough edges of their schoolroom establishment, prettifying the Sunday school so that the judge will get an enhanced sense of what is normal there. Such sugarcoating of reality is a particular object of Twain's contempt, and it is exactly what he does *not* want his fiction to do. Twain is committed to realism, to depicting the everyday world with all its irregularities and imperfections. In fact, Twain's penchant for roughness and variation makes his satire more tender and compassionate than it might otherwise be.

QUOTATIONS

4. Tom was a glittering hero once more—the pet of the old, the envy of the young. His name even went into immortal print, for the village paper magnified him. There were some that believed he would be President, yet, if he escaped hanging.

The community's assessment of Tom in Chapter 24, after his testimony against Injun Joe, implicitly acknowledges the close relationship between Tom's misbehavior and his heroism. If Tom had not sneaked out at night to carouse in the cemetery with Huck, he would never have been present to witness Dr. Robinson's murder—as by all rights he should not have been. Tom's consistently bold and risky behavior puts him in the position to save the day. Distinguishing himself from the conventional, run-of-the-mill behavior that is accepted as the standard in his community is an achievement that cuts both ways, as it makes Tom exceptional in both the good and the bad sense: an extreme character like his is bound to lead either to greatness or to ignominy; as the town puts it, he either will become president or hang.

5.   Huck Finn's wealth and the fact that he was now under
the Widow Douglas's protection introduced him into
society—no, dragged him into it, hurled him into it—and
his sufferings were almost more than he could bear. The
widow's servants kept him clean and neat, combed and
brushed. . . . He had to eat with knife and fork; he had to
use napkin, cup, and plate; he had to learn his book, he
had to go to church; he had to talk so properly that speech
was become insipid in his mouth; whithersoever he turned,
the bars and shackles of civilization shut him in and bound
him hand and foot.

This passage from Chapter 35 is perhaps the clearest description of
the way Huck's life changes after the Widow Douglas takes him in.
Though told by the narrator rather than by Huck himself, the passage nevertheless renders the situation as it appears through Huck's
eyes. This technique—rendering a limited, childish point of view as
though it were objective—is one Twain uses throughout the novel to
help us identify with the boys more than with the adults of the town.
Much of the force of Twain's heavily nostalgic narrative comes from
the way it tugs at the memories most adult readers have stored away,
however deeply, of what it was like to be a child. We are thus able
to view the events of the novel from a double perspective: from a
child's point of view and from a wider perspective that sees the limi-
tations of that view and, most likely, its charm as well. The ordinary
quality of the things the Widow Douglas compels Huck to do is
meant to shock us out of our own assumptions. We realize afresh
how unorthodox Huck's life has actually been. This realization in
turn forces us to contemplate more intently the way a life of nor-
malcy could feel like a prison after a life of such radical freedom.

QUOTATIONS

KEY FACTS

FULL TITLE
The Adventures of Tom Sawyer

AUTHOR
Samuel Clemens, usually known by his pen name, Mark Twain

TYPE OF WORK
Novel

GENRE
Concerned with Tom's personal growth and quest for identity, *The Adventures of Tom Sawyer* incorporates several different genres. It resembles a bildungsroman, a novel that follows the development of a hero from childhood through adolescence and into adulthood. The novel also resembles novels of the picaresque genre, in that Tom moves from one adventurous episode to another. *The Adventures of Tom Sawyer* also fits the genres of satire, frontier literature, folk narrative, and comedy.

LANGUAGE
English

TIME AND PLACE WRITTEN
1874–1875; Hartford, Connecticut

DATE OF FIRST PUBLICATION
The novel appeared in England in June 1876, and six months later in the United States.

NARRATOR
An adult who views the adult world critically and looks back on the sentiments and pastimes of childhood in a somewhat idealized manner, with wit and also with nostalgia

POINT OF VIEW
The narrator narrates in the third person, with a special insight into the workings of the boyish heart and mind.

TONE
Satirical and nostalgic

TENSE
>   Past

SETTING (TIME)
>   Not specified, but probably around 1845

SETTING (PLACE)
>   The fictional town of St. Petersburg, Missouri (which resembles Twain's hometown of Hannibal)

PROTAGONIST
>   Tom Sawyer

MAJOR CONFLICT
>   Tom and Huck perceive their biggest struggle to be between themselves and Injun Joe, whose gold they want and whom they believe is out to kill them. Conflict also exists between Tom and his imaginative world and the expectations and rules of adult society.

RISING ACTION
>   Tom and Huck's witness of Dr. Robinson's murder; the search for the boys' bodies in the river when they escape to Jackson's Island; Tom's testimony at Muff Potter's trial; Tom and Huck's accidental sighting of Injun Joe at the haunted house; Tom and Becky's entrapment in the cave

CLIMAX
>   Huck overhears Injun Joe's plan to kill the Widow Douglas, and Tom encounters Injun Joe when he and Becky are stranded in the cave.

FALLING ACTION
>   Huck gets help from the Welshman and drives Injun Joe away from the Widow Douglas; Tom avoids conflict with Injun Joe and navigates himself and Becky out of the cave; Judge Thatcher seals off the cave, causing Injun Joe to starve to death; Tom and Huck find Injun Joe's treasure; Huck is adopted and civilized by the Widow Douglas.

THEMES
>   Moral and social maturation; society's hypocrisy; freedom through social exclusion; superstition in an uncertain world

KEY FACTS

MOTIFS

Crime; trading; the circus; "showing off"

SYMBOLS

The cave; the storm; the treasure; the village

FORESHADOWING

When he is frustrated by his fight with Becky, Tom declares his intention to become a pirate, foreshadowing his later excursion to Jackson's Island; Tom's great fear of Injun Joe foreshadows his later encounters with him; Tom's obsession with the oath he and Huck have taken never to speak about Dr. Robinson's murder foreshadows the fact that Tom will later break the oath and testify at Muff Potter's trial.

Study Questions

1. *How does Tom Sawyer change over the course of the story?*

The beginning of the novel shows Tom as a crafty, intelligent, and imaginative boy with excellent theatrical skills and an intuitive understanding of human nature. He expends his immense personal resources mainly on tricks and games—on getting into and then out of trouble in the real world and on elaborate flights of make-believe. He rarely takes anything seriously and seems to have no real conflicts.

The murder of Dr. Robinson is the first serious conflict to present itself in the story, and we see Tom begin to change after he witnesses it. His anxiety and guilt about Muff Potter's fate are plain in the scenes in which he tries to get Huck to reconsider their vow to secrecy. The decision he finally makes is independent by every indication, however. Tom decides to follow his conscience despite the ties that have bound him—his devotion to loyalty, superstition, and his personal safety.

Tom's disregard of his own interest prepares us for even greater transformations in his character. In taking Becky Thatcher's punishment, Tom exercises a preliminary heroism that conforms more to his storybook notions of chivalry and romance than it resolves a real conflict. His chivalry and competence while he and Becky are trapped in the cave, however, represent a more meaningful, adult version of the same lesson in self-sacrifice and concern for others. When Tom encourages Huck to return to the Widow Douglas's house in the final scene, his transformation is complete. Though he does not cease to be a playful and fun-loving character, he has learned through experiencing various dangers and mistakes to value the resources of home and community and to accept a certain measure of outside authority.

2.   *Analyze the character of Aunt Polly and her relationship to Tom.*

Though Tom and Aunt Polly position themselves as foes within the family—he as the troublemaker and she as the disciplinarian—they are actually similar in many ways. Aunt Polly has a humorous appreciation for Tom's cleverness and his antics that often prevents her from disciplining him as severely as she should. At times, she tries to beat him at his own game—for example, when she tries to trick him into confessing that he has gone swimming instead of to school. But, despite their superficially adversarial relationship, there is a real bond of loyalty and love between Tom and Aunt Polly. The worst punishment she can inflict on Tom is to cry or be hurt by his behavior. Similarly, the misdeed of Tom's that she reacts to most strongly is his inconsiderate allowance of her suffering when she thinks that he is dead. Tom spies on the scene of the family's mourning for him, and Aunt Polly finds the piece of bark with the message on it in Tom's pocket—each character is extremely gratified by discovering indisputable evidence of the other's affection. Aunt Polly thus embodies a more positive kind of authority than the rest of adult society because her strictness is balanced with real love and concern. Like Tom, she exhibits the truly positive elements of social relations, without all the hypocrisy and insincerity.

3. *What role do alcohol and images of drunkenness play in the novel?*

For a children's adventure story, *The Adventures of Tom Sawyer* is rich in references to drinking and alcohol. Huck's father and Muff Potter are both alcoholics. Tom and Huck accidentally find whiskey in the back rooms of the Temperance Tavern. Tom joins the Cadets of Temperance organization but then quits because it is too stringent. Even Aunt Polly dabbles innocently in alcohol, which is likely the main ingredient of the "patent medicines" she administers to Tom (and which he, in turn, administers to the cat).

This obsession with alcohol fits into the larger themes of the novel because *The Adventures of Tom Sawyer* is in many ways a story about pushing the limits of acceptable social behavior. Muff Potter is more or less tolerated, largely because he does very little harm. Huck's father, Pap, is a more ambiguous character because his debauchery has serious implications for his son. The issue of drinking also allows Twain to expand on the charges of hypocrisy that he levels against so many social proceedings. The temperance violations offer a prime example of the kind of transgressions people may hide under a surface of respectability. Even the schoolmaster, who should be a role model for the children, turns out to be a heavy drinker. Twain's focus on performances, charlatanism, and various kinds of false advertising finds another instance in the quack medicines of which Aunt Polly is so enamored. Unlike those who pretend to be sober but are not, Aunt Polly would probably be horrified to realize what she is actually getting for her money.

How to Write
Literary Analysis

The Literary Essay: A Step-by-Step Guide

When you read for pleasure, your only goal is enjoyment. You might find yourself reading to get caught up in an exciting story, to learn about an interesting time or place, or just to pass time. Maybe you're looking for inspiration, guidance, or a reflection of your own life. There are as many different, valid ways of reading a book as there are books in the world.

When you read a work of literature in an English class, however, you're being asked to read in a special way: you're being asked to perform *literary analysis*. To analyze something means to break it down into smaller parts and then examine how those parts work, both individually and together. Literary analysis involves examining all the parts of a novel, play, short story, or poem—elements such as character, setting, tone, and imagery—and thinking about how the author uses those elements to create certain effects.

A literary essay isn't a book review: you're not being asked whether or not you liked a book or whether you'd recommend it to another reader. A literary essay also isn't like the kind of book report you wrote when you were younger, where your teacher wanted you to summarize the book's action. A high school- or college-level literary essay asks, "How does this piece of literature actually work?" "How does it do what it does?" and, "Why might the author have made the choices he or she did?"

The Seven Steps
No one is born knowing how to analyze literature; it's a skill you learn and a process you can master. As you gain more practice with this kind of thinking and writing, you'll be able to craft a method that works best for you. But until then, here are seven basic steps to writing a well-constructed literary essay:

1. *Ask questions*
2. *Collect evidence*
3. *Construct a thesis*

4. Develop and organize arguments
5. Write the introduction
6. Write the body paragraphs
7. Write the conclusion

---

1. ASK QUESTIONS

When you're assigned a literary essay in class, your teacher will often provide you with a list of writing prompts. Lucky you! Now all you have to do is choose one. Do yourself a favor and pick a topic that interests you. You'll have a much better (not to mention easier) time if you start off with something you enjoy thinking about. If you are asked to come up with a topic by yourself, though, you might start to feel a little panicked. Maybe you have too many ideas—or none at all. Don't worry. Take a deep breath and start by asking yourself these questions:

- **What struck you?** Did a particular image, line, or scene linger in your mind for a long time? If it fascinated you, chances are you can draw on it to write a fascinating essay.

- **What confused you?** Maybe you were surprised to see a character act in a certain way, or maybe you didn't understand why the book ended the way it did. Confusing moments in a work of literature are like a loose thread in a sweater: if you pull on it, you can unravel the entire thing. Ask yourself why the author chose to write about that character or scene the way he or she did and you might tap into some important insights about the work as a whole.

- **Did you notice any patterns?** Is there a phrase that the main character uses constantly or an image that repeats throughout the book? If you can figure out how that pattern weaves through the work and what the significance of that pattern is, you've almost got your entire essay mapped out.

- **Did you notice any contradictions or ironies?** Great works of literature are complex; great literary essays recognize and explain those complexities. Maybe the title (*Happy Days*) totally disagrees with the book's subject matter (hungry orphans dying in the woods). Maybe the main character acts one way around his family and a completely different way around his friends and associates. If you can find a way to explain a work's contradictory elements, you've got the seeds of a great essay.

At this point, you don't need to know exactly what you're going to say about your topic; you just need a place to begin your exploration. You can help direct your reading and brainstorming by formulating your topic as a *question,* which you'll then try to answer in your essay. The best questions invite critical debates and discussions, not just a rehashing of the summary. Remember, you're looking for something you can *prove or argue* based on evidence you find in the text. Finally, remember to keep the scope of your question in mind: is this a topic you can adequately address within the word or page limit you've been given? Conversely, is this a topic big enough to fill the required length?

GOOD QUESTIONS

"Are Romeo and Juliet's parents responsible for the deaths of their children?"

"Why do pigs keep showing up in LORD OF THE FLIES?"

"Are Dr. Frankenstein and his monster alike? How?"

BAD QUESTIONS

"What happens to Scout in TO KILL A MOCKINGBIRD?"

"What do the other characters in JULIUS CAESAR *think about Caesar?"*

"How does Hester Prynne in THE SCARLET LETTER *remind me of my sister?"*

---

2. COLLECT EVIDENCE

Once you know what question you want to answer, it's time to scour the book for things that will help you answer the question. Don't worry if you don't know what you want to say yet—right now you're just collecting ideas and material and letting it all percolate. Keep track of passages, symbols, images, or scenes that deal with your topic. Eventually, you'll start making connections between these examples and your thesis will emerge.

Here's a brief summary of the various parts that compose each and every work of literature. These are the elements that you will analyze in your essay, and which you will offer as evidence to support your arguments. For more on the parts of literary works, see the Glossary of Literary Terms at the end of this section.

ELEMENTS OF STORY   These are the *what*s of the work—what happens, where it happens, and to whom it happens.

- **Plot:** All of the events and actions of the work.
- **Character:** The people who act and are acted upon in a literary work. The main character of a work is known as the *protagonist.*
- **Conflict:** The central tension in the work. In most cases, the protagonist wants something, while opposing forces (antagonists) hinder the protagonist's progress.
- **Setting:** When and where the work takes place. Elements of setting include location, time period, time of day, weather, social atmosphere, and economic conditions.
- **Narrator:** The person telling the story. The narrator may straightforwardly report what happens, convey the subjective opinions and perceptions of one or more characters, or provide commentary and opinion in his or her own voice.
- **Themes:** The main idea or message of the work—usually an abstract idea about people, society, or life in general. A work may have many themes, which may be in tension with one another.

ELEMENTS OF STYLE   These are the *how*s—how the characters speak, how the story is constructed, and how language is used throughout the work.

- **Structure and organization:** How the parts of the work are assembled. Some novels are narrated in a linear, chronological fashion, while others skip around in time. Some plays follow a traditional three- or five-act structure, while others are a series of loosely connected scenes. Some authors deliberately leave gaps in their works, leaving readers to puzzle out the missing information. A work's structure and organization can tell you a lot about the kind of message it wants to convey.
- **Point of view:** The perspective from which a story is told. In *first-person point of view,* the narrator involves him or herself in the story. ("I went to the store"; "We watched in horror as the bird slammed into the window.") A first-person narrator is usually the protagonist of the work, but not always. In *third-person point of view,* the narrator does not participate

LITERARY ANALYSIS

in the story. A third-person narrator may closely follow a specific character, recounting that individual character's thoughts or experiences, or it may be what we call an *omniscient* narrator. Omniscient narrators see and know all: they can witness any event in any time or place and are privy to the inner thoughts and feelings of all characters. Remember that the narrator and the author are not the same thing!

- **Diction:** Word choice. Whether a character uses dry, clinical language or flowery prose with lots of exclamation points can tell you a lot about his or her attitude and personality.

- **Syntax:** Word order and sentence construction. Syntax is a crucial part of establishing an author's narrative voice. Ernest Hemingway, for example, is known for writing in very short, straightforward sentences, while James Joyce characteristically wrote in long, incredibly complicated lines.

- **Tone:** The mood or feeling of the text. Diction and syntax often contribute to the tone of a work. A novel written in short, clipped sentences that use small, simple words might feel brusque, cold, or matter-of-fact.

- **Imagery:** Language that appeals to the senses, representing things that can be seen, smelled, heard, tasted, or touched.

- **Figurative language:** Language that is not meant to be interpreted literally. The most common types of figurative language are *metaphors* and *similes,* which compare two unlike things in order to suggest a similarity between them— for example, "All the world's a stage," or "The moon is like a ball of green cheese." (Metaphors say one thing *is* another thing; similes claim that one thing is *like* another thing.)

---

3. CONSTRUCT A THESIS

When you've examined all the evidence you've collected and know how you want to answer the question, it's time to write your thesis statement. A *thesis* is a claim about a work of literature that needs to be supported by evidence and arguments. The thesis statement is the heart of the literary essay, and the bulk of your paper will be spent trying to prove this claim. A good thesis will be:

- **Arguable.** "*The Great Gatsby* describes New York society in the 1920s" isn't a thesis—it's a fact.

LITERARY ANALYSIS

- **Provable through textual evidence**. "*Hamlet* is a confusing but ultimately very well-written play" is a weak thesis because it offers the writer's personal opinion about the book. Yes, it's arguable, but it's not a claim that can be proved or supported with examples taken from the play itself.

- **Surprising**. "Both George and Lenny change a great deal in *Of Mice and Men*" is a weak thesis because it's obvious. A really strong thesis will argue for a reading of the text that is not immediately apparent.

- **Specific**. "Dr. Frankenstein's monster tells us a lot about the human condition" is *almost* a really great thesis statement, but it's still too vague. What does the writer mean by "a lot"? *How* does the monster tell us so much about the human condition?

GOOD THESIS STATEMENTS

Question: In *Romeo and Juliet*, which is more powerful in shaping the lovers' story: fate or foolishness?

Thesis: "Though Shakespeare defines Romeo and Juliet as 'star-crossed lovers' and images of stars and planets appear throughout the play, a closer examination of that celestial imagery reveals that the stars are merely witnesses to the characters' foolish activities and not the causes themselves."

Question: How does the bell jar function as a symbol in Sylvia Plath's *The Bell Jar*?

Thesis: "A bell jar is a bell-shaped glass that has three basic uses: to hold a specimen for observation, to contain gases, and to maintain a vacuum. The bell jar appears in each of these capacities in *The Bell Jar*, Plath's semi-autobiographical novel, and each appearances marks a different stage in Esther's mental breakdown."

Question: Would Piggy in *The Lord of the Flies* make a good island leader if he were given the chance?

Thesis: "Though the intelligent, rational, and innovative Piggy has the mental characteristics of a good leader, he ultimately lacks the social skills necessary to be an effective one. Golding emphasizes this point by giving Piggy a foil in the charismatic Jack, whose magnetic personality allows him to capture and wield power effectively, if not always wisely."

4. Develop and Organize Arguments

The reasons and examples that support your thesis will form the middle paragraphs of your essay. Since you can't really write your thesis statement until you know how you'll structure your argument, you'll probably end up working on steps 3 and 4 at the same time.

There's no single method of argumentation that will work in every context. One essay prompt might ask you to compare and contrast two characters, while another asks you to trace an image through a given work of literature. These questions require different kinds of answers and therefore different kinds of arguments. Below, we'll discuss three common kinds of essay prompts and some strategies for constructing a solid, well-argued case.

Types of Literary Essays

- **Compare and contrast**

    Compare and contrast the characters of Huck and Jim in The Adventures of Huckleberry Finn.

    Chances are you've written this kind of essay before. In an academic literary context, you'll organize your arguments the same way you would in any other class. You can either go *subject by subject* or *point by point*. In the former, you'll discuss one character first and then the second. In the latter, you'll choose several traits (attitude toward life, social status, images and metaphors associated with the character) and devote a paragraph to each. You may want to use a mix of these two approaches—for example, you may want to spend a paragraph a piece broadly sketching Huck's and Jim's personalities before transitioning into a paragraph or two that describes a few key points of comparison. This can be a highly effective strategy if you want to make a counterintuitive argument—that, despite seeming to be totally different, the two objects being compared are actually similar in a very important way (or vice versa). Remember that your essay should reveal something fresh or unexpected about the text, so think beyond the obvious parallels and differences.

- **Trace**

    Choose an image—for example, birds, knives, or eyes—and trace that image throughout Macbeth.

    Sounds pretty easy, right? All you need to do is read the play, underline every appearance of a knife in *Macbeth,* and then list them in your essay in the order they appear, right? Well, not exactly. Your teacher doesn't want a simple catalog of examples. He or she wants to see you make *connections* between those examples—that's the difference between summarizing and analyzing. In the *Macbeth* example above, think about the different contexts in which knives appear in the play and to what effect. In *Macbeth,* there are real knives and imagined knives; knives that kill and knives that simply threaten. Categorize and classify your examples to give them some order. Finally, always keep the overall effect in mind. After you choose and analyze your examples, you should come to some greater understanding about the work, as well as your chosen image, symbol, or phrase's role in developing the major themes and stylistic strategies of that work.

- **Debate**

  Is the society depicted in 1984 *good for its citizens?*

  In this kind of essay, you're being asked to debate a moral, ethical, or aesthetic issue regarding the work. You might be asked to judge a character or group of characters (*Is Caesar responsible for his own demise?*) or the work itself (*Is* JANE EYRE *a feminist novel?*). For this kind of essay, there are two important points to keep in mind. First, don't simply base your arguments on your personal feelings and reactions. Every literary essay expects you to read and analyze the work, so search for evidence in the text. What do characters in *1984* have to say about the government of Oceania? What images does Orwell use that might give you a hint about his attitude toward the government? As in any debate, you also need to make sure that you define all the necessary terms before you begin to argue your case. What does it mean to be a "good" society? What makes a novel "feminist"? You should define your terms right up front, in the first paragraph after your introduction.

  Second, remember that strong literary essays make contrary and surprising arguments. Try to think outside the box. In the *1984* example above, it seems like the obvious answer would be no, the totalitarian society depicted in Orwell's novel is *not* good for its citizens. But can you think of any arguments for the opposite side? Even if your final assertion is that the novel depicts a cruel, repressive, and therefore harmful society, acknowledging and responding to the counterargument will strengthen your overall case.

5. Write the Introduction

Your introduction sets up the entire essay. It's where you present your topic and articulate the particular issues and questions you'll be addressing. It's also where you, as the writer, introduce yourself to your readers. A persuasive literary essay immediately establishes its writer as a knowledgeable, authoritative figure.

An introduction can vary in length depending on the overall length of the essay, but in a traditional five-paragraph essay it should be no longer than one paragraph. However long it is, your introduction needs to:

- **Provide any necessary context.** Your introduction should situate the reader and let him or her know what to expect. What book are you discussing? Which characters? What topic will you be addressing?

- **Answer the "So what?" question.** Why is this topic important, and why is your particular position on the topic noteworthy? Ideally, your introduction should pique the reader's interest by suggesting how your argument is surprising or otherwise counterintuitive. Literary essays make unexpected connections and reveal less-than-obvious truths.

- **Present your thesis.** This usually happens at or very near the end of your introduction.

- **Indicate the shape of the essay to come.** Your reader should finish reading your introduction with a good sense of the scope of your essay as well as the path you'll take toward proving your thesis. You don't need to spell out every step, but you do need to suggest the organizational pattern you'll be using.

Your introduction should not:

- **Be vague.** Beware of the two killer words in literary analysis: *interesting* and *important*. Of course the work, question, or example is interesting and important—that's why you're writing about it!

- **Open with any grandiose assertions.** Many student readers think that beginning their essays with a flamboyant statement such as, "Since the dawn of time, writers have been fascinated with the topic of free will," makes them sound important and commanding. You know what? It actually sounds pretty amateurish.

- **Wildly praise the work.** Another typical mistake student writers make is extolling the work or author. Your teacher doesn't need to be told that "Shakespeare is perhaps the greatest writer in the English language." You can mention a work's reputation in passing—by referring to *The Adventures of Huckleberry Finn* as "Mark Twain's enduring classic," for example—but don't make a point of bringing it up unless that reputation is key to your argument.

- **Go off-topic.** Keep your introduction streamlined and to the point. Don't feel the need to throw in all kinds of bells and whistles in order to impress your reader—just get to the point as quickly as you can, without skimping on any of the required steps.

6. WRITE THE BODY PARAGRAPHS

Once you've written your introduction, you'll take the arguments you developed in step 4 and turn them into your body paragraphs. The organization of this middle section of your essay will largely be determined by the argumentative strategy you use, but no matter how you arrange your thoughts, your body paragraphs need to do the following:

- **Begin with a strong topic sentence.** Topic sentences are like signs on a highway: they tell the reader where they are and where they're going. A good topic sentence not only alerts readers to what issue will be discussed in the following paragraph but also gives them a sense of what argument will be made *about* that issue. "Rumor and gossip play an important role in *The Crucible*" isn't a strong topic sentence because it doesn't tell us very much. "The community's constant gossiping creates an environment that allows false accusations to flourish" is a much stronger topic sentence— it not only tells us *what* the paragraph will discuss (gossip) but *how* the paragraph will discuss the topic (by showing how gossip creates a set of conditions that leads to the play's climactic action).

- **Fully and completely develop a single thought.** Don't skip around in your paragraph or try to stuff in too much material. Body paragraphs are like bricks: each individual

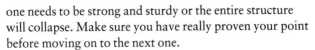

one needs to be strong and sturdy or the entire structure will collapse. Make sure you have really proven your point before moving on to the next one.

- **Use transitions effectively.** Good literary essay writers know that each paragraph must be clearly and strongly linked to the material around it. Think of each paragraph as a response to the one that precedes it. Use transition words and phrases such as *however, similarly, on the contrary, therefore,* and *furthermore* to indicate what kind of response you're making.

---

7. WRITE THE CONCLUSION

Just as you used the introduction to ground your readers in the topic before providing your thesis, you'll use the conclusion to quickly summarize the specifics learned thus far and then hint at the broader implications of your topic. A good conclusion will:

- **Do more than simply restate the thesis.** If your thesis argued that *The Catcher in the Rye* can be read as a Christian allegory, don't simply end your essay by saying, "And that is why *The Catcher in the Rye* can be read as a Christian allegory." If you've constructed your arguments well, this kind of statement will just be redundant.

- **Synthesize the arguments, not summarize them.** Similarly, don't repeat the details of your body paragraphs in your conclusion. The reader has already read your essay, and chances are it's not so long that they've forgotten all your points by now.

- **Revisit the "So what?" question.** In your introduction, you made a case for why your topic and position are important. You should close your essay with the same sort of gesture. What do your readers know now that they didn't know before? How will that knowledge help them better appreciate or understand the work overall?

- **Move from the specific to the general.** Your essay has most likely treated a very specific element of the work—a single character, a small set of images, or a particular passage. In your conclusion, try to show how this narrow discussion has wider implications for the work overall. If your essay on *To Kill a Mockingbird* focused on the character of Boo Radley, for example, you might want to include a bit in your conclusion about how he fits into the novel's larger message about childhood, innocence, or family life.

- **Stay relevant.** Your conclusion should suggest new directions of thought, but it shouldn't be treated as an opportunity to pad your essay with all the extra, interesting ideas you came up with during your brainstorming sessions but couldn't fit into the essay proper. Don't attempt to stuff in unrelated queries or too many abstract thoughts.

- **Avoid making overblown closing statements.** A conclusion should open up your highly specific, focused discussion, but it should do so without drawing a sweeping lesson about life or human nature. Making such observations may be part of the point of reading, but it's almost always a mistake in essays, where these observations tend to sound overly dramatic or simply silly.

A+ Essay Checklist

Congratulations! If you've followed all the steps we've outlined above, you should have a solid literary essay to show for all your efforts. What if you've got your sights set on an A+? To write the kind of superlative essay that will be rewarded with a perfect grade, keep the following rubric in mind. These are the qualities that teachers expect to see in a truly A+ essay. How does yours stack up?

- ✓ Demonstrates a thorough understanding of the book
- ✓ Presents an original, compelling argument
- ✓ Thoughtfully analyzes the text's formal elements
- ✓ Uses appropriate and insightful examples
- ✓ Structures ideas in a logical and progressive order
- ✓ Demonstrates a mastery of sentence construction, transitions, grammar, spelling, and word choice

Suggested Essay Topics

1. *Analyze the relationship between Tom and Huck, paying close attention to their trip to the graveyard and their hunt for the treasure.*

2. *Analyze Tom's relationship to the other boys his age, paying close attention to the whitewashing scene and the scenes at school.*

3. *Discuss how Twain uses satire in the Sunday school scene.*

4. *Trace Tom's courtship of Becky. In what ways is their romance adultlike? In what ways is it childish?*

5. *Discuss Twain's portrayal of the town's authority figures, especially Judge Thatcher, Mr. Dobbins, and the minister.*

6. *Analyze Twain's portrayal of Injun Joe. Does Twain want us to feel sympathy for Injun Joe? How can you tell?*

7. *Analyze the relationship between the adults and children of St. Petersburg. Focus especially on the adult reaction to Tom Sawyer.*

A+ Student Essay

> A bildungsroman is a novel about the education and maturing of its main character. To what extent can *The Adventures of Tom Sawyer* be classified as a bildungsroman?

At first glance, *The Adventures of Tom Sawyer* seems to be a thoroughly traditional bildungsroman. After all, the novel shows Tom's transformation from a naughty boy into a hero praised by the adults in his community. But the adults in Twain's novel are no more mature than the children they're raising. Twain does not narrate a change in Tom's personality, but rather a change in the foolish adults' perception of Tom. *The Adventures of Tom Sawyer* reveals itself to be an unabashed celebration of the subversive spirit of childhood—the exact opposite of a bildungsroman.

On the surface, the novel presents a tale of one boy's moral development. In a famous early scene, Tom flaunts his skills as a prankster by convincing other children to whitewash his aunt's fence for him. He doesn't feel any remorse, even though his game hurts other people. He acts in a self-absorbed way again when he runs away from home, allowing his friends and neighbors to conclude that he has died before making a surprise appearance at his own funeral. But later events in the novel—Tom's decision to save Becky, and his offer of half his money to Huck Finn—convince the adults that Tom has reformed and turned into a man. Read this way, Twain's novel fits the definition of a bildungsroman perfectly.

Throughout the novel, however, Twain plants evidence to suggest that the adult characters have poor judgment or are otherwise untrustworthy. For example, Tom manages to easily dupe his caregiver, the slave-owning Aunt Polly, by yelling, "Look behind you!" and jumping out the window. Another representative of the adult world, Huck's father, is both a negligent parent and a drunk. The august Judge Thatcher sees Tom as a "fine, manly little fellow," despite the fact that all the children in Sunday school know that Tom has cheated his way to the coveted Bible prize. Dr. Robinson attempts to dig up a corpse at night, Injun Joe is a murderer, and Mr. Dobbins whips students without proof of their misbehavior. A popular meeting spot for the adults, Temperance Tavern, serves alcohol in a backroom. Given the abundant examples of the adults' shortsightedness and hypocrisy, it seems doubtful that Twain wants to present adulthood as a condition to aspire to.

Tom begins and ends the novel as a well meaning but mischievous boy. When Judge Thatcher praises him and says that he would be a good candidate for the National Military Academy and a career in law, he laughably misinterprets Tom's character. Despite Judge Thatcher's optimistic daydreaming, the end of the novel contains many examples of Tom's lingering boyishness. He wouldn't have had the opportunity to save Becky Thatcher from the cave, for example, if he hadn't led her into it in the first place. In his final scene, though Tom has become wealthy and received praise from both the Judge and Aunt Polly, he remains a sly and inventive child, envisioning himself as the leader of a robber gang that will find Injun Joe's buried treasure.

It's not surprising that *The Adventures of Tom Sawyer* has become a beloved children's novel, because the novel contrasts the intelligence and good humor of children with the poor judgment of adults. Twain conceals his subversive message within the familiar structure of a bildungsroman, in which a boy gets into trouble and redeems himself before his superiors. But Tom does not turn into the obedient citizen the adults want him to be: At the end of the novel, he still dreams of causing chaos in a robbers' gang. His story celebrates the freedom, mischief, and excitement of youth, and suggests that children shouldn't hurry to grow up and become adults.

GLOSSARY OF LITERARY TERMS

ANTAGONIST

The entity that acts to frustrate the goals of the *protagonist*. The antagonist is usually another *character* but may also be a non-human force.

ANTIHERO / ANTIHEROINE

A *protagonist* who is not admirable or who challenges notions of what should be considered admirable.

CHARACTER

A person, animal, or any other thing with a personality that appears in a *narrative*.

CLIMAX

The moment of greatest intensity in a text or the major turning point in the *plot*.

CONFLICT

The central struggle that moves the *plot* forward. The conflict can be the *protagonist*'s struggle against fate, nature, society, or another person.

FIRST-PERSON POINT OF VIEW

A literary style in which the *narrator* tells the story from his or her own *point of view* and refers to himself or herself as "I." The narrator may be an active participant in the story or just an observer.

HERO / HEROINE

The principal *character* in a literary work or *narrative*.

IMAGERY

Language that brings to mind sense-impressions, representing things that can be seen, smelled, heard, tasted, or touched.

MOTIF

A recurring idea, structure, contrast, or device that develops or informs the major *themes* of a work of literature.

NARRATIVE

A story.

NARRATOR

The person (sometimes a *character*) who tells a story; the *voice* assumed by the writer. The narrator and the author of the work of literature are not the same person.

PLOT

The arrangement of the events in a story, including the sequence in which they are told, the relative emphasis they are given, and the causal connections between events.

POINT OF VIEW

The *perspective* that a *narrative* takes toward the events it describes.

PROTAGONIST

The main *character* around whom the story revolves.

SETTING

The location of a *narrative* in time and space. Setting creates mood or atmosphere.

SUBPLOT

A secondary *plot* that is of less importance to the overall story but may serve as a point of contrast or comparison to the main plot.

SYMBOL

An object, *character,* figure, or color that is used to represent an abstract idea or concept. Unlike an *emblem,* a symbol may have different meanings in different contexts.

SYNTAX

The way the words in a piece of writing are put together to form lines, phrases, or clauses; the basic structure of a piece of writing.

THEME

A fundamental and universal idea explored in a literary work.

TONE

The author's attitude toward the subject or *characters* of a story or poem or toward the reader.

VOICE

An author's individual way of using language to reflect his or her own personality and attitudes. An author communicates voice through *tone, diction,* and *syntax.*

LITERARY ANALYSIS

A Note on Plagiarism

Plagiarism—presenting someone else's work as your own—rears its ugly head in many forms. Many students know that copying text without citing it is unacceptable. But some don't realize that even if you're not quoting directly, but instead are paraphrasing or summarizing, *it is plagiarism* unless you cite the source.

Here are the most common forms of plagiarism:

- Using an author's phrases, sentences, or paragraphs without citing the source
- Paraphrasing an author's ideas without citing the source
- Passing off another student's work as your own

How do you steer clear of plagiarism? You should *always* acknowledge all words and ideas that aren't your own by using quotation marks around verbatim text or citations like footnotes and endnotes to note another writer's ideas. For more information on how to give credit when credit is due, ask your teacher for guidance or visit www.sparknotes.com.

Review & Resources

Quiz

1. How does Tom trick his friends into helping him whitewash the fence?

    A. He offers them marbles.
    B. He promises to go swimming with them when the job is done.
    C. He tells them Aunt Polly wants them to help.
    D. He convinces them that the job is fun.

2. Why do Tom and Huck first go to the graveyard?

    A. To dig up a body
    B. To charm away warts
    C. To dig for buried treasure
    D. To kill a cat

3. What is Jackson's Island?

    A. A small island in the middle of the Mississippi River
    B. A tavern in town
    C. An amusement park in St. Louis
    D. The setting of Tom's favorite adventure book

4. Who is Sid?

    A. Aunt Polly's boyfriend
    B. Tom's cocker spaniel
    C. Tom's younger half-brother
    D. Tom's father

5. What does Injun Joe do after Tom testifies against him?

    A. He denies his guilt.
    B. He flees out the window.
    C. He terrorizes the boys.
    D. He kills Muff Potter.

6.   What insect does Tom release in church?

    A.   A tick
    B.   A grasshopper
    C.   A ladybug
    D.   A pinch-bug

7.   Who is blamed for the murder of Dr. Robinson?

    A.   Muff Potter
    B.   Injun Joe
    C.   Hoss Williams
    D.   Tom Sawyer

8.   What does Tom do to win a Bible in Sunday school?

    A.   He memorizes 2,000 Bible verses.
    B.   He takes the blame for someone else's misdeed.
    C.   He trades with the other children for their tickets.
    D.   He testifies at Muff Potter's trial.

9.   What does Huck do outside Tom's window to summon him to their midnight adventures?

    A.   He barks like a dog.
    B.   He meows like a cat.
    C.   He crows like a rooster.
    D.   He hoots like an owl.

10.   Who is the first of the boys to suggest abandoning the pirating expedition?

    A.   Tom Sawyer
    B.   Huckleberry Finn
    C.   Ben Rogers
    D.   Joe Harper

11.   Who is unaffected by the revival that sweeps through town?

    A.   Tom Sawyer, who is sick at the time
    B.   Huck Finn, who has no parents to supervise his religious education
    C.   Sid, who is always mean and selfish
    D.   Mary, who is too good to need reforming

12. What day is bad luck for hunting buried treasure?

    A. Halloween
    B. Examination Day
    C. Friday
    D. Tuesday

13. Why does Huck not go on the picnic?

    A. Because he has promised to keep watch for Injun Joe
    B. Because he has not been invited
    C. Because he cannot stand girls
    D. Because he is afraid of boats

14. What happens when Tom and Joe learn to smoke?

    A. They win Huck's friendship.
    B. They get a whipping from Aunt Polly.
    C. They are expelled from Sunday school.
    D. They get sick.

15. Who decides to have McDougal's Cave bolted shut?

    A. Judge Thatcher
    B. Mrs. Harper
    C. Injun Joe
    D. Tom Sawyer

16. What will become of the treasure Huck and Tom find?

    A. It will be returned to its rightful owners.
    B. It will be spent on a memorial for Injun Joe.
    C. It will be invested for the boys.
    D. It will be donated to the Sunday school.

17. Who is the only person to hug Huck when the three boys return for the funeral?

    A. Tom Sawyer
    B. Becky Thatcher
    C. Muff Potter
    D. Aunt Polly

REVIEW & RESOURCES

18. Who adopts Huck Finn at the end of the novel?

    A.   Aunt Polly
    B.   The Widow Douglas
    C.   Judge Thatcher
    D.   Muff Potter

19. Whom does Tom encounter in the cave?

    A.   Judge Thatcher
    B.   Injun Joe
    C.   Huck Finn
    D.   Muff Potter

20. What keeps Injun Joe from finding Tom and Huck hidden upstairs in the haunted house?

    A.   They jump out the window.
    B.   A noise frightens Injun Joe away.
    C.   The staircase begins to crumble.
    D.   The treasure distracts him.

21. Why does Injun Joe want revenge on the Widow Douglas?

    A.   Because her husband once punished and humiliated him
    B.   Because she never returned his affections when they were younger
    C.   Because she made a racist comment about Native Americans
    D.   Because she will not give him any ice cream

22. Whom does Tom suspect of spilling ink on his spelling book?

    A.   Becky Thatcher
    B.   Huck Finn
    C.   Alfred Temple
    D.   Himself

23. What is Huck most afraid of when he and Tom return to the cave to find the treasure?

    A. Injun Joe's ghost
    B. Being locked in
    C. A band of robbers
    D. Bats

24. Who doesn't believe Tom's claim that he dreamed about things that occurred at home while he was pirating on Jackson's Island?

    A. Aunt Polly
    B. Cousin Mary
    C. Becky Thatcher
    D. Sid

25. What does Tom find behind door No. 2 at the Temperance Tavern?

    A. Milk and cookies
    B. Whiskey and Injun Joe
    C. Buried treasure
    D. A dead cat

ANSWER KEY

1: D; 2: B; 3: A; 4: C; 5: B; 6: D; 7: A; 8: C; 9: B; 10: D; 11: A; 12: C; 13: B; 14: D; 15: A; 16: C; 17: D; 18: B; 19: B; 20: C; 21: A; 22: D; 23: A; 24: D; 25: B

SUGGESTIONS FOR FURTHER READING

CLEMENS, SAMUEL L. *Mark Twain's (Burlesque) Autobiography.* Madison, WI: University of Wisconsin Press, 1990.

EMERSON, EVERETT H. *Mark Twain: A Literary Life.* Philadelphia: University of Pennsylvania Press, 2000.

EVANS, JOHN D. *A* TOM SAWYER *Companion: An Autobiographical Guided Tour with Mark Twain.* Lanham, MD: University Press of America, 1993.

GERBER, JOHN C. "Introduction" and "Sources for Characters." In Mark Twain, *The Adventures of Tom Sawyer.* Berkeley, CA: University of California Press, 1982.

HOWELLS, WILLIAM DEAN. *"The Adventures of Tom Sawyer."* In *My Mark Twain.* Mineola, NY: Dover Publications, 1997.

HUTCHINSON, STUART, ed. *Mark Twain:* TOM SAWYER *and* HUCKLEBERRY FINN. New York: Columbia University Press, 1999.

NORTON, CHARLES A. *Writing* TOM SAWYER. Jefferson, NC: McFarland, 1983.

SCHARNHORST, GARY, ed. *Critical Essays on* THE ADVENTURES OF TOM SAWYER. New York: G. K. Hall & Company, 1993.